Sexual Accusations *and* SOCIAL TURMOIL

What Can Be Done

BY

Jules H. Masserman, M.D.

Past President, American Psychiatric Association
Honorary Life President, World Association for Social Psychiatry

WITH CONTRIBUTIONS BY
Christine McGuire Masserman
Associate Director Emerita, Medical Education
University of Illinois College of Medicine

Prologue by Claire Burch
Poet, Author

Epilogue by Barbara W. Stackler
Counselor-at-law

Regent Press
Oakland, California
1994

Manufactured in the United States.
Design by Sara Glaser

Regent Press
6020-A Adeline
Oakland, CA 94608

ISBN: 0-916147-42-8 paperback
ISBN: 0-916147-43-6 hardcover

Library of Congress Cataloging-in-Publication Data

Masserman, Jules Hymen, 1905-
    Sexual accusations and social turmoil / by Jules H. Masserman ;
with contributions by Christine McGuire Masserman ; prologue by
Claire Burch ; epilogue by Barbara W. Stackler.
      p. cm.
    Includes bibliographical references.
    ISBN 0-916147-43-6 : $26.95. — ISBN 0-916147-42-8 (pbk.) : $14.95
    1. Sex crimes—United States. 2. Malicious accusation—United States.
3. Psychotherapist and patient—United States—Case studies.
4. Masserman, Jules Hymen, 1905- . 5. Psychiatrists—
United States—Biography. 6. Noel, Barbara. 7. Psychotherapy
patients—United States—Biography. I. Masserman, Christine
McGuire. II. Title
HV6592.M37 1994
362.88'3'092--dc20
    [B]   94-2247
                                            CIP

Sexual Accusations *and* SOCIAL TURMOIL

What Can Be Done

Table of Contents

APPENDIX

Dedication

*My wife Christine, with characteristic grace,
declined to be duly credited as co-author
of this book, yet her wisdom imbues every page.
To her, as have been all my previous writings,
this book is dedicated.*

JHM

Brief Preview

The author, an internationally renowned psychiatrist, was accused by a patient of a sexual assault. As related in Part One of the book, immediate medical, laboratory and police investigation disproved the charge, but the attendant publicity initiated a decade of personal, professional and social stresses typical of those experienced by many other innocent victims of similar accusations. The author's wife Christine, herself a distinguished educator, describes the couple's ordeals, and discusses measures that would be helpful to other families similarly traumatized in this time of psychosocial turmoil.

Part Two elaborates a background theme: our erotically obsessed society which, as in medieval times, seeks individuals on whom to project its guilts. In illuminating perspectives, topical chapters trace the origin, biologic basis and evolution of sexuality, its relationships to other fundamental human motivations, and its historical, cultural and religious expressions. Of special concern are the serious juristic and social problems related to current associations of sexuality and violence. The concluding chapters of Part Two deal with existing problems and possible solutions in the early cultural training and later education of our youth in the interest of the welfare and redirected creativity of succeeding generations. A Keynote Chord envisions this future.

Part Three then spans the transitions from youth to aging as exemplified by the author's personal experiences.

Every effort has been made to keep the text clear and informative. Illustrative documents and supplementary comments are assembled in an Appendix.

The book is dedicated to the many thousands of individuals who have been, or will be, falsely accused of sexual transgressions, and to all readers who are increasingly and intelligently concerned about our current cultural travails, and who wish to improve and, in an ideal sense, humanize our juristic and social systems.

Jules H. Masserman, M.D.
Chicago, Illinois, 1993

PROLOGUE
A Culture Obsessed
Claire Burch

In 1969 and 1970, I was in correspondence with Dr. Jules
Masserman when he was one of a group of eminent psychiatrists kind enough to read and comment on my book on home
care in emotional disturbance, *Stranger In The Family,* as it
developed. His remarks were always on target. I had read several of his own books, *A Psychiatric Odyssey* and *Biodynamic
Roots of Human Behavior,* and experienced them as dense, fascinating and brilliant.

He was happily married, he was totally focused on his work
and his spare time went toward such classic sublimations as
musical composition, lectures and travel. I was therefore deeply
troubled to learn that in 1984 he had been accused of a sexual
assault on a patient. Eventually I was to learn that I was only
one of many who found the accusation impossible to believe.

I was privileged to have access to the actual evidence which
definitively disproved the allegation. In addition I was introduced through his new book to an enlightened overview of the
epidemic of witch hunts characteristic of today's terrified, yet
sex-obsessed and victimizing society. My hunch was that as

Victorianism followed syphilis before a cure was found, so a new prurience is following the all too real AIDS concern. In addition I couldn't help but note the explosion of enormous, financially rewarding malpractice suits against doctors, particularly psychiatrists.

These accusations are accelerating all the time. We read of them against pop stars, famous Hollywood directors/writers, day care providers for children, the President of the United States, and even a cardinal of the Catholic Church—a rash of name-calling that means almost certain headlines and puts the impossible burden of proving themselves innocent on anyone so named. The wave of accusals that has become fashionable and profitable, prompts pop books and magazines filled with sensational sleaze, "fun" reading for the curious and salacious.

Much damage has been done. Years, sadly, cannot be relived.

I am glad that at least the Massermans now finally see, after almost a decade, an official vindication in their lifetime. It is to their credit that instead of succumbing to the tragedy that engulfed them, they completed this book and hopefully will cast light on the problem for others, by reverting to their lifetime research, reflection and writing, presently exploring the sexual crisis of our society. Their book is valuable for many reasons beyond the personal incidents described.

The purpose of *Sexual Accusations and Social Turmoil* is to explore reality. When the reader has noted facts, not fantasy and confused perception, once again it will be clear that in our frantic subculture, many injustices occur. To keep such events from continuing, careful scrutiny of our culture and our judicial system is indicated. We must distinguish true accusals from false and vicious ones. It is ironic that of all the burning issues of mental health Dr. Masserman has spent his life clarifying and exploring, his last has had to focus on the socially important problems involved in false allegations of sexual misconduct, with millions of dollars in lawsuits often at stake.

Convinced that the accusation against Dr. Masserman had been made as the result of a dream, a fantasy or an hallucination, I am concerned as to what can be done to correct such blurring of body boundaries that leads to the tidal wave of sexual accusations we are seeing today.

The Sixties had its problems also, but we are now trapped in a Lycra and nylon web of escalating malpractice horror stories that, unless checked by the kind of rueful, truthful overview this book reveals, catches us all in some kind of "absence seizure" of the heart, a deja vu of another society in history, Victorianism, and the tight-lipped repressions it encourages.

Justice Delayed

In a certified letter dated July 23, 1993, the Chairman of the Ethical Relations Committee of the Chicago Medical Society notified me that charges had been filed against me. Citing "findings" of the American Psychiatric Association with regards to "incompetent medical practice" and "sexual improprieties," made in response to a patient's unsupported allegations some nine years previously, the CMS complaint "accused" me specifically of "violation of ethical conduct as defined by the Chicago Medical Society" and of "acts of serious misconduct which bring discredit to either the Chicago Medical Society or the medical profession," for either of which a "member of the... Society may be censured, placed on probation, suspended, or expelled."

I was subsequently summoned to an official hearing of the Committee on October 20, 1993, at which the attested evidence presented in this book disproving the charges that I had transgressed professional or ethical standards was thoroughly examined.

On October 27, 1993, I received a letter on the stationery of the Chicago Medical Society in which the Chairman of the Committee stated that the Committee "acquits [me] of the charges."

I replied:

Dear Dr. Brackett:

The decision of the CMS Ethical Relations Committee has confirmed my faith in the eventual probity, balanced judgment and essential humanity of the vast majority of my medical colleagues.

With heartfelt appreciation.

Sincerely,

(signed) Jules H. Masserman, M.D.

PART ONE

Sexual Accusations

Chapter 1

Allegations and Initial Defenses

I, Jules Masserman, retired Co-Chairman of Behavioral Sciences at Northwestern University, had conducted an ethical and successful psychiatric and psychoanalytic practice for forty years, had published a dozen books and hundreds of articles, had been elected president of the American Psychiatric Association and four other professional societies, had received both the Albert Lasker Scientific Research and the Sigmund Freud Psychoanalytic Awards along with many other similar national and international honors.* *Then, in my eightieth year, Barbara Noel, a patient, accused me of sexually assaulting her.*

Immediate medical, gynecologic, laboratory and police investigations proved her charge false; however, the attendant publicity initiated many years of personal and social travails. These were borne with what patience and resilience I could muster from my training and earlier experience as described in Chapter 11. However, these stresses became intolerable when, in 1992, Ms. Kathleen Watterson, on paid assignment, wrote a book entitled *You Must Be Dreaming,* garishly jacketed and

---

* Chapter 11 presents a more extensive account for readers seeking biographic determinants.

salaciously promoted for wide distribution (see Chapter 4). In it Ms. Noel asserted, in effect, that I had frequently "drugged and raped" her over many years, that I had similarly abused other patients, and that I had been expelled from my professional associations and had lost my right to practice.

Thus, eight years after Ms. Noel's original complaint in 1984, I was again subjected to a vicious misuse of a public medium for crass monetary gains—an abuse that many others of variable prominence suffer in our culture. In my case, I had the following options:

One. Legally relieved by Ms. Noel's actions, of the last vestige of previous ethical restraints of confidentiality, I could utilize many invitations to appear on national radio and TV programs in which I could cite attested data that would completely destroy her credibility. However, as this would be descending to her level of conduct—and would violate my Hippocratic pledge never to harm a patient whatever his or her behavior—it was an unacceptable option.

Two. I could, as advised by one attorney, sue Ms. Watterson, Ms. Noel and their publisher for libelous defamation of character, citing incontrovertible evidence as to the falsity of their allegations. Such suits are increasingly effective; however in my case they would involve additional years of expensive and exhausting litigation, and even a favorable verdict, though clearly justified, would not compensate for the injuries and injustices long since imposed (Chapters 3 and 4).

Three. I could write my own book about the Noel episode, reviewing the events clearly and objectively—and I hope, interestingly—as significant of many other ominous cultural, moral and legal aberrations in our sex-obsessed, covertly guilty and reactively victimizing society (Chapter 5 and 8).

This is that book. The narrative follows.

During the afternoon of September 20, 1984, Barbara Noel, my patient for eighteen years, telephoned to request an emergency consultation. An interview early the following morning revealed that she was excessively anxious, depressed and potentially suicidal in reaction to an accumulation of adversities, and needed prompt symptomatic relief and interim alleviation of stress. As described below, I therefore employed an effective therapeutic procedure, termed an amytal interview, to facilitate the analysis and at least partial resolution of her seemingly overwhelming problems. At its termination she expressed gratitude for my care and counsel, clearer insight, and anticipated improvement in her career and interpersonal relationships. I then departed for obligations at my university after arranging for my office nurse, Ms. Peggy Karas, who had been present in the office throughout the morning, to oversee Ms. Noel's restful relaxation until she was ready to leave.

On my return to the office that afternoon, Ms. Karas reported that she had found Ms. Noel fully alert, responsive and resting comfortably a half hour and again one hour after my departure, and had conversed with her pleasantly about her next week's appointment. However, despite a friendly but noncommittal interim call to Ms. Karas, Ms. Noel did not appear for her next appointment, and did not call to cancel it. When this occurred the following week, I became concerned that she had reverted to one of her favorite modes of escape from depression: locking herself in her room and drinking herself into successive stupors.

I had rescued her from this form of semi-suicide by calling her home during several previous life crises, and therefore did so during the afternoon of October 12. In response to an inquiry about her welfare, her reply, confused and almost inarticulate, was to give me the telephone number of a "Dr. McMany" who was currently "taking care" of her. As professionally required, I called the number, and was informed by a pleasant-voiced individual who identified himself as Patrick Mahoney, that he was an attorney who had been engaged by Ms. Noel to enter suit against me for assault.

Shocked and partly unbelieving, I nevertheless did what I had never before been required to do: fully inform the attorney of my insurance firm of the possibility of an impending suit— thus initiating an era of legal correspondence here representatively reproduced for optimum objectivity.

Report to My Insurance Company (in which some facts had to be stated)

To: Mr. E. Michael Kelly, Attorney-at-Law
From: Jules H. Masserman, M.D.
Subject: Ms. Barbara Noel

History. Ms. Barbara Noel has been a patient of mine irregularly for over eighteen years, during which time I have helped her through her second marriage, frequent bouts of alcoholism, extramarital sexual liaisons (one with a homosexual physician also my patient), disappointments in her operatic aspirations (she now sings only occasionally with a dance band), and recurrently deep depressive and panic states, often with suicidal preoccupations. In therapy I elicited and analyzed her unresolved attachments to her father, guided her to a more realistic career and improved interpersonal relationships. I prescribed Antabuse to control her alcoholism, but avoided all other oral drugs to prevent new addictions; instead, when her depressive or agitated states were excessively severe, I utilized minimal injections of 0.20 to 0.25 gm. of sodium amytal during special interviews technically designed to elicit and alleviate Ms. Noel's deeper concerns and enhance her receptivity to helpful guidance. Fortunately, there were years during which Ms. Noel was cooperative with medical, analytic and supportive psychotherapy, and no amytal interviews were required, but when utilized they were invariably followed by mental and physical relief and expressions of gratitude. In her case as in others, whenever it was necessary for me to leave the office for lecture or other engagements before a patient, still under mild relaxation, was ready to leave, I always confirmed that his or her general responsiveness, breathing, pulse and blood pressure were normal, and instructed my office nurse to check these periodically before the patient's departure.

Financial. Ms. Noel's fees were kept at less than my usual rate per session, because of her recurrent unemployment, urgent needs and statements of limited resources. She has always paid promptly, and continued to express gratitude for her sometimes erratic but generally progressive improvement.

Interview on September 21, 1984. Ms. Noel stated that she was severely depressed on many counts: among them, her ill-fitting dentures, her unsatisfactory singing and the rejections of a song she had written for publication, gloom over other financial and professional failures, her resumption of excessive drinking, and angry melancholy over her variously related but conflicting sexual liaisons with George (half her age), John (a magazine writer), Rich (a music arranger), Frank (her bandmaster), Owen (a radio broadcaster), and Marshall, an academic to whom she was especially attracted.* She had requested but had been denied an amytal session for several months, but to avert an impending panic, one now appeared advisable.

The Amytal Interview. September 21, 1984. About 9:30 AM.[(Appendix, Reference 1)] After an initial discussion of her concerns described above, Ms. Noel, as instructed on previous occasions, rolled the sleeve on her left arm to the elbow and reclined on a cot in a room equipped for neurological exami-

---

* To preserve their interests I here cite only the given names of persons fully identified by Ms. Noel as significant in her life; other deletions and minor alterations in this letter are here made for purposes of clarity and in accord with special ethical considerations.

nations, which adjoined both my office and that of Ms. Peggy Karas, my nurse-secretary. After determining that her breathing, pulse and blood pressure were normal, I also used the arm cuff as a gentle tourniquet and injected 0.20 gm. of sodium amytal in sterile 10% solution in a cubital vein, over a period of fifteen minutes, with repeated checks of pulse and respiration. During this interval and for another thirty minutes, Ms. Noel again talked about missing her father's admiration and support, deplored her lack of appreciation as a singer and composer, resented the hostilities and jealousies in her dance band, and reasserted her disappointments in all men, including her former husbands, her current divorce attorney, and her coteries of present lovers, especially Owen and now Marshall. As in other interviews I reinforced previous counsel as to how she could emancipate herself from her father's ambitions for her as a prima donna, and recultivate on more reasonable grounds Marshall, John or some other desirable marital partner for the financial and social security she sought, while also pursuing a more attainable musical career as a singer, teacher and composer of popular ballads. Her complaints became less strident, her mood lighter, and her comments more rational over the ensuing half hour. She thanked me for a sense of relief and restored purpose, helped me remove the cuff from her arm, and remained communicative. I returned to my office to write an IBM consultation report, rechecked Ms. Noel's condition and found her content, pleasant and responsive to questions. At about 11:45 AM I instructed her, as on previous occasions, to remain as long as she wished and to leave when ready, but not to drive, to take drugs or to drink alcoholic beverages for at least another six hours. She agreed, thanked me again, and I left for an appointment at Northwestern.

Follow-up. Several days later Ms. Noel called Ms. Karas to say that she would be out of town but would call for an appointment on her return. However, when she did not do so for another two weeks I asked Ms. Karas to reach her so I could make sure that she was not again, as on several previous occasions, in an alcoholic stupor, a suicidal depression or some other serious difficulty. Since Ms. Noel made no response to the messages Ms. Karas left with her answering service, I felt professionally obligated to call her home at about 4:10 PM on October 12, 1984. Ms. Noel answered in an indistinct, strained, high-pitched voice that she had been advised not to talk to me and referred me to a "Dr. McMany." I called the number she provided in the hope that she was under proper medical care, but was courteously informed that "Dr. McMany" was an attorney who "wanted to be friendly" but who had filed suit against me for "malpractice and assault" about which I would learn next week.

If the alleged "assault" means an unwanted amytal injection, Ms. Noel had requested this on many previous occasions, including once from my office associate, Dr. Victor Uribe (see below), when I was out of town for an extended period. If she alleges sexual assault, she involves both my former and my current office nurses as accomplices to a crime, and implies that I would risk losing not only my profession but also, knowing of Ms. Noel's various sexual adventures, my own and my wife's health and life.

I trust I need not assure you, as her eighteen-year confidence in me would also indicate, that I have always treated Ms. Noel considerately and ethically and did so on the occasion in question, as Ms. Karas can confirm.

(Signed) Jules H. Masserman, M.D.

But I was now enmeshed in the American legal system. Debra Davy, a young attorney in the firm of Hinshaw, Culbertson, et al., who succeeded Mr. Kelly in the Noel suit, assured me that Mr. Mahoney, after investigating Ms. Noel's allegations, had petitioned the Court and had been granted permission to withdraw as her advocate, and that another similarly ethical female attorney had also refused to represent her. A few weeks later, however, I was informed that Ms. Noel had finally found a lawyer, Mr. Ken Cunniff, who, as assisted by an associated psychologist, would sue me on the contingency that he receive one third of any financial settlement he could obtain.

A startling manifestation of this development was that several women patients currently in therapy with me began reporting that Ms. Noel had telephoned and visited them bearing offers of large financial awards if they would join her suit on the grounds that, being myself a drug addict, I had not only drugged and raped them, but had also poisoned Savilla Laird, my former nurse-secretary who had served me faithfully for thirty-two years and who presumably knew about my "transgressions." My patients' prevailing impressions: Ms. Noel had either been drinking or had become mentally deranged.

There ensued a three-year melange of telephone calls (often introduced with the cautionary code word "Personal!"), reams of letters (darkly and ominously marked "PERSONAL AND CONFIDENTIAL") and a seemingly endless succession of consultations, conferences and audio- or videotaped depositions, in some of which I was cross-examined either patronizingly or with studied contempt by Ms. Noel's lawyers who, while practicing their pretrial posturing, also condoned having Ms. Noel scream "Rape!" at me.

Co-complainants. Eventually, two former patients, here respectively designated Ms. Doe and Ms. Roe to protect their identity, were apparently persuaded to consult Ms. Noel's attorneys with complaints about which I was never fully informed. I had guided Ms. Doe from almost complete irresponsibility, through her bar examination, to a position in a legal firm where she became engaged to a wealthy client, and I had helped her friend Ms. Roe through serious drug, sexual and single parent conflicts. Both had completed therapy over a year previously, with expressions of gratitude and written agreements to pay delinquent accounts. The last I saw of either of them was when, on special invitation to Mrs. Masserman and myself, we attended the wedding of Ms. Doe to her former client. After the ceremony she, her father (a prominent physician), her groom, and Ms. Roe (her maid of honor) had publicly paid tribute to my past counseling as having "brought about this happy occasion." Following the wedding, the only other communications with Ms. Doe and Ms. Roe were letters sent to them by my secretary reminding them of their written pledges to pay the fees still due when they completed therapy. I received no reply nor any notice of complaints about their treatment.

Cumulative Evidence

During these many months the insurance attorney, Ms. Davy, obtained and attested relevant data that further convinced her of my innocence, including the following.

As to events preceding the alleged attack, an unsolicited letter from N.S., a prominent industrialist, that read in part as follows:

In the summer of 1984, Ms. Billie Laird, who was a secretary to Dr. Masserman for over 30 years, died shortly after returning home from a vacation. I made arrangements to attend the funeral with two friends of mine who also knew Billie quite well. One was Mrs. J.S. and the other, Barbara Noel.

…Sometime during the morning…the name of Dr. Masserman came up during a conversation among the three of us.…It may have been Mrs. S.…who brought up Dr. Masserman's name as being one of the most incisive, dedicated and effective practitioners in his field.

As a result of that comment, Barbara Noel turned to me

and said the following: That she knew that he was really one of the best practitioners of psychiatry around today and that there sure was a great difference between many of these practitioners in the field of human behavior. She said that Dr. Masserman was incisive, dedicated, and a first rate physician superbly trained in the practice of psychiatric medicine.... She went on to relate that at sometime... she had ...withdrawn from treatment...to see... a psychologist and found that the quality of treatment she had been originally exposed to by Dr. Masserman was so much better...that she realized, for her own sake, that she should...re-enter therapy with Dr. Masserman and so, that is what she did.

(Signed) N.S.,
Executive Vice-President

As to Ms. Noel's appreciation of an amytal session when under excessive stress, which I also rechanneled into analytic and supportive therapy whenever possible, Ms. Davy secured this verbatim report from my colleague, Dr. Victor Uribe:

I am the office associate psychiatrist to Jules H. Masserman, M.D.; Ms. Peggy Karas is our full-time registered nurse and secretary. On Wednesday, August 15, 1984, Ms. Karas received a phone call from Ms. Barbara Noel, a longtime patient of Dr. Masserman. According to Ms. Karas, Ms. Noel told her that she wanted me to give her sodium amytal that day or before the weekend. I took the phone call and Ms. Noel told me that she wanted me to give her sodium amytal, as Dr. Masserman had given it to her once in awhile. She added that she knew that Dr. Masserman was out of town until August 20 and that I was available to cover for him if she needed help during his absence.

I asked her to explain to me the reasons for which she thought she needed it right away. She said that it was not necessary for her to go into details and that all she wanted was the sodium amytal. I told her that I needed to know at least her present symptoms and any pertinent and related current situations before I could give any opinion about her request. She said she was considering to make some decisions before the weekend, was feeling tense and wanted to relax. I asked her to describe symptoms, feelings, ideas and anything else that she was experiencing. She said that she was just preoccupied and tense but nothing else.

I then explained to Ms. Barbara Noel that I did not consider sodium amytal necessary at that time. I told her that if she wanted to talk further with me about her present tension and preoccupations, that I would be glad to give her an appointment but that it did not mean that I was going to give her sodium amytal unless I would consider it therapeutically indicated after a face-to-face clinical evaluation. She said that she was feeling less preoccupied after talking with me, gave me her thanks for my comments and added that she would try to resolve the mentioned [difficulties] by herself.

I made myself available to her through my 24-hour answering service. I encouraged her to call me if she needed or to call Dr. Masserman on his return on August 20, 1984.

Throughout the phone consultation, Ms. Barbara Noel expressed to me her deepest gratitude and trust toward Dr. Masserman for his always available and longtime professional and effective help. Ms. Noel did not call me again.

(Signed) Victor M. Uribe, M.D.

As to the alleged attack itself, Attorney Davy was also able to diagram and attest to the site and circumstances of the alleged assault. My examining room is far from soundproof, and has thin, readily opened doors: one to my office and the secretary and waiting room, the other directly into an outside corridor lined by other offices. Yet Ms. Noel, though admittedly fully conscious and unrestrained, uttered no protests against what she claimed was a brutal intrusion, summoned no help from the waiting room or adjacent offices and made no efforts to leave after the alleged "attack." Instead, she was relaxed, placid and fully cooperative during post-amytal, follow-up interviews with me and later with Nurse Karas.

As to Ms. Noel's fantasy that when she did leave I "was sitting at my desk," "invited [her] to lunch," and other such "memories" of the event as described in Ms. Watterson's book, Ms. Davy recorded the following sworn testimony of my nurse-secretary:

> As instructed by Dr. Masserman, I checked Ms. Noel's condition in the examining room after he left. I found her resting comfortably and responding reassuringly to my inquiries. At about 1:00 PM I left the office for a short time and on my return found Ms. Noel had left.
> (Signed) Peggy Karas, R.N.

As to Ms. Noel's admission in Ms. Watterson's book that she may have been "dreaming," Ms. Davy also secured the office notes of Dr. Stuart Abel, Ms. Noel's gynecologist, recorded when she consulted him shortly after she left my office.[Appendix, Reference 2]

> **Sep 21 1984,** Has been seeing a psychiatrist for yrs. Gets shots of sodium amytal for rest and "new start." —Says she was either raped or dreamt she was raped while under the influence of amytal in her psychiatrist's office. Wanted me to tell her. I did not examine her but sent her to Olsen Emergency Room stat where patient could be followed. She said she knew where it was and left promptly.

A similar statement, indicating that Ms. Noel had spontaneously volunteered that she may have been "hallucinating," was recorded in his office notes by Dr. Coleman Seskind, her internist, whom she consulted immediately after leaving my office on September 21, 1984.[Appendix, Reference 3]

The police officer, Thomas Fleming, who examined Ms. Noel at Northwestern Emergency Clinic shortly after the alleged attack, likewise noted in his signed report that Ms. Noel "stated to R/O [Responding Officer] that she was unable to determine whether [the] incident was a dream or reality." (Appendix, Reference 4)

None of the Emergency physicians who then examined Ms. Noel had found any pudendal hair, seminal residues, gynecologic contusions, or cytologic, hematologic, serologic or other evidence either on Ms. Noel or on her underclothing to support any allegation of a sexual assault.(Appendix, Reference 5)

Finally, Crime Detective J. Kelly, by reputation an especially conscientious and efficient officer, after recontacting Ms. Noel, concluded his follow-up police report submitted some two weeks later with this notation: (Appendix, Reference 6)

> The victim related that she did not want the offender confronted with the allegation because there was a possibility that she dreamed the incident while she was unconscious. She related she was going to confer with her attorney.
>
> On 27 Sep 84 victim was recontacted and related that she has conferred with her attorney and she is not going to pursue the matter criminally at this time. As the victim refuses to prosecute at this time [I] request that this case be EX-CLEARED at this time.

Rational Conclusion. From the above evidence and as inferable from Ms. Noel's later confused and self-contradictory depositions (available but too voluminous to be reproduced here), there had been no "sexual assault" on Ms. Noel on September 21, 1984 or at any other time.

Irrational Consequences. Many more years of tension and travail yet to be described.

Chapter 2

Unsettling Settlements

As the evidence outlined in Chapter 1 accumulated, Ms. Davy kept assuring me that no reasonable judge or jury would consider me guilty of any professional or ethical transgression. Nevertheless, sessions with Ms. Noel's lawyers continued, and some two years after the alleged assault, senior attorneys at Hinshaw, Culbertson et al. informed me that they now had the following choices:

"We could go to trial and very probably win." However, that would entail three or more years of conferences, depositions, pretrial hearings and other strenuous confrontations. The firm was aware that my wife, Christine, was now almost completely bedridden by a progressive arthritis in both hip joints and that, on the basis of increasing urinary difficulties and alarming laboratory reports, I was scheduled for a series of operations to arrest or remove a prostate cancer. The lawyers assigned to my defense therefore feared that at my age (then eighty-two) the juristic stresses they anticipated would seriously endanger my welfare and adequate care for Christine, and that even if I survived the trial, a highly unlikely but always possible adverse verdict that exceeded my insurance coverage would seriously complicate my ordeal.

Alternatively, Hinshaw-Culbertson could conclude an out-of-court settlement at low cost and with no publicity or admission of guilt, close the case, and free me of further concerns—a course they would recommend.

I had dealt with many legal issues as officer or president of various organizations but never any that involved Christine's or my own physical and financial welfare. In the present instance the second option, as recommended by a prestigious law firm, seemed reasonable. Though I never signed the legally required Consent to Settle Form, and assuming (as it turned out, mistakenly) that I would have an opportunity to review and approve any settlement agreement, I wrote a letter to Ms. Davy to the following effect:

> In view of the special contingencies outlined in a recent conference with yourself and your colleagues, I can accept their recommendations for an out-of-court arrangement under the following conditions: that there is no admission of any culpability on my part; that the case is finally closed; and that there be no publicity about the settlement.

Since no court decision could have had consequences more devastating than what ensued, that letter was a serious misjudgment. Despite what Ms. Davy later described as an unrecorded "gentlemen's agreement" with Kenneth Cunniff, Ms. Noel's attorney, a heavily headlined and sensationally phrased article in the *Chicago Tribune* of January 6, 1987, informed the public that Jules Masserman, a "world famous psychiatrist," whose career was now ruined, had paid $250,000 to Barbara Noel and two other former patients to compensate them for sexual assaults. Nor did the *Tribune* article omit an implicit invitation to Dr. Masserman's other patients who might like to profit similarly; the name and address of Kenneth Cunniff, Ms. Noel's "winning" attorney, were conveniently supplied.

I had thought that after the prognosis of my imminent death in medical school, as described in Chapter 11, I had achieved a fair balance of thought and emotion, and that this balance had been sufficiently stabilized by my subsequent training and personal analysis to withstand later threats. But I was wrong. The widely broadcast attack on my integrity and accomplishments was excessively traumatic.

Psychologically, I experienced an angry disillusionment about our culture and its legal system, particularly the morally vacuous cupidity that some lawyers transfer to their equally unprincipled clients; socially, I moved under a cloud of depression and embarrassment; physically, I spent nearly sleepless nights and lost weight and energy. Indeed, all of these reactions might have become seriously counterproductive were it not for the unimpaired confidence of current and former patients, sincere communications of support from students, colleagues and many friends, invitations to present the keynote addresses at the Annual Meetings of the Society of Biological Psychiatry and the American Academy of Psychoanalysis, the acceptance of two book manuscripts (*Psychiatric Consultations* and *Adolescent Sexuality*) for publication, and other assurances of maintained status, respect and prestige. And none was as steadying and heartening as the understanding, love and encouragement constantly offered by Christine, soon to be more deeply needed than ever.

Chapter 3

Retirement

A few months after the appearance of the *Tribune* article, two brusque and burly representatives of the Illinois Department of Professional Regulation came to my office. Reason for their visit: Barbara Noel had complained to the Department that nearly three years previously I had, in the now familiar phrase, "drugged and raped her," so they were there to check on my "store of drugs." Since they had no copy of the complaint, no official directives from the Department and no search warrant, I could have, as I was later informed, more or less politely asked them to leave. However, since I had meticulously followed all national and state regulations with regard to controlled substances, I unlocked a small cabinet, let them examine and take notes about my sparse store of standard anxiety-relieving drugs (Tranxene, Valium, Xanax and Propanolol), six tablets of Tylenol #3 for acute pain, a vial of sodium amytal and one of adrenalin for cardiac or other office emergencies. The inquisitors departed without comment. However, a subsequent communication from the Department informed me that, since the *Tribune* article had also indicated that I might be unfit for medical practice, Departmental regulations required that I either appear at a new series of hearings to disprove Ms. Noel's charges or that, in view of my more than forty years of commendable service, I retire from practice voluntarily.

Fortunately the latter option resonated with what I had intended to do. My health had deteriorated: hearing had become impaired, one eye was astigmatic and the other half blinded by a cataract, and renewed cystoscopic and laboratory tests had indicated that urgent surgery was necessary for suspected cancer. But these considerations faded into insignificance compared with my deep concern for Christine who, after a long series of orthopedic examinations I had arranged for her, now lay at home virtually bedridden awaiting bilateral hip implants at my university. I had, indeed, long planned to retire from teaching and practice at age eighty, and I had already served notice that I would not be renewing my office lease.

In sum, I therefore chose to discontinue practice on the specific condition that the official records would indicate that there had been no violation of any ethical or other Departmental regulation. I completed therapy for my remaining patients or referred them for competent care elsewhere, closed my office and brought my books and files to my library and study at home.

The American Psychiatric Association (APA)

Peace, however, was not to be.

In a letter dated March 15, *1987,* sent to David R. Hawkins, Chairman of the Ethics Committee of the Illinois Psychiatric Society (IPS), Ms. Noel reiterated her complaint that I had sexually assaulted her in *1984,* adding that she and her attorney were soliciting former patients to join in their complaint. Specific passages read as follows:

"There is a pattern at work [by Dr. Masserman] that continued from the first amytal session....I have contacted the involved women whom I know.... Mr. Cunniff has offered to call the women who have chosen to remain anonymous."

I was therefore summoned to attend a hearing of the IPS on November 16, 1989. In accord with IPS regulations I could have chosen not to attend on several grounds. For one, the Committee had long exceeded the mandatory nine-month limit for investigating a transgression that was alleged to have occurred some five years previously; for another, I had been shown no copies of Ms. Noel's current complaint or other relevant documents. However, I did not take advantage of these or many other procedural errors which, as past president of the IPS as well as of the APA, I clearly recognized; instead, I appeared before the Committee to clear any doubts as to my personal and professional conduct.

Contrary to still another IPS requirement that an accused member have full opportunity to confront and question the accuser, neither Ms. Noel nor her attorney attended the hearing; therefore, all I could do was present documented evidence that I had treated Ms. Noel over a period of eighteen years in full accord with high professional standards, and that there had not been any ethical transgression on September 21, 1984, or at any other time.

After the hearing, I waited in an anteroom for half an hour until Dr. Donald Langsley, co-chairman of the Committee, informed me that, whereas *the Committee could, indeed, not find that I had committed any sexual transgressions,* there were "indications" *(unspecified)* of a "questionable pattern" of treating patients (a charge no other patient had made to the Committee) that needed "further investigation." Therefore, there would be a second hearing to which—ominous warning—I "had better bring my lawyer."

This initiated a Kafkaesque period of concerned bewilderment: the Committee could not find me guilty of the only charge against me—that of a sexual assault, so it would now investigate an unspecified "pattern" of presumed misconduct of which, to my knowledge, I had not been charged by anyone other than the Committee. Shades of Torquemada and the Witches' Hammer in the twentieth century? Only later did I learn directly from the minutes of Committee meetings of their repeated—and unsuccessful—efforts to elicit additional charges against me from other patients, *de novo.*

It seemed advisable to follow the only lead I had been given: I engaged Barbara Stackler, a highly regarded expert in such pseudojuristic inquisitions, discussed the Noel data with her and her husband (also a prominent defense attorney) and arranged for both to be present at the Committee's second hearing. That session was held some eight months later at the Committee headquarters, and proved even less credible than the previous one. Ms. Stackler had submitted a petition to dismiss the sole complaint against me on the ground that the Committee had now exceeded, by nearly four years, the maximum time limit officially set by the IPS for final action on any complaint. Ms. Stackler's petition was arbitrarily denied, without consideration.

Then, contrary to an APA regulation that the accused receive prior written notice of the name of any complainant and the full text of his or her allegations, a Ms. C.I., who had terminated treatment more than a decade earlier, was sworn in to make a "complaint" about which I had not been informed. However, as quoted from the official transcript of the hearing, she immediately stated:

> "I have not filed a complaint. I was invited... to come to this hearing as a witness [for Ms. Noel]... [by] Dr. Langsley." (Transcript, pp. 79, 87)

Under gentle but revealing questioning by Ms. Stackler, Ms. C.I. admitted that she had never met Ms. Noel prior to this hearing, had no direct knowledge of her alleged assault some six years earlier, and so could not serve as a witness regarding the only issue properly before the Committee. Whereupon, despite her protests to the contrary, the Committee's attorney, Mr. Robert Graham, ruled Ms. C.I. to be an "undeclared complainant," and directed her to continue her testimony in that capacity (Transcript, p. 65). Ms. C.I. then testified that after reading the *Tribune* article about the large award made to Ms. Noel "this light bulb went off in my head" (Transcript, p. 84), and that she had then contacted Ms. Noel's attorneys in the hope of similar profit. Her testimony then became so self-contradictory that she asked to be dismissed.

When Ms. Noel took the complainant's chair, she restated her version of the "assault" on September 21, 1984, in lurid, uninterrupted detail and continued with additional allegations to the effect that other patients had been similarly abused, hence, the source of the Committee's notion at the previous meeting of a reprehensible "pattern of mistreatment."

After some thirty minutes of this litany, Ms. Stackler began her examination with the usual introductory queries about Ms. Noel's background, but before she could proceed to the factual evidence against Ms. Noel's sole complaint to the Committee, namely, that she had been "drugged and raped" six years previously, the co-chairman ruled that Ms. Stackler had only a few minutes left of the half hour arbitrarily assigned for cross-examination. Despite this unexpected restraint, Ms. Stackler elicited from Ms. Noel admissions that I had treated her considerately, courteously and very helpfully during eighteen years of therapy, that (in Ms. Noel's recorded words) she "had no memory" of any sexual or other transgression prior to the alleged assault on September 21, 1984, and that she had volunteered to three physicians and an assigned police crime detective that it may have been a "dream" or an "hallucination." At this point the Committee's chair terminated Ms. Stackler's examination and directed me to "state my case."

Since Ms. Noel's accusations had released me from the restraints of confidentiality, I had prepared a list of questions as to her neurotic behavior in childhood and adolescence, her alcoholism, her sexual promiscuity throughout her marriages, and other queries relevant to her lack of stability and credibility. The questions were also phrased so as to reveal her improvements in behavior under analytic, supportive and referred group therapies, with rare amytal interviews utilized only as indicated for the relief of deep depressive, panic or suicidal reactions to exceptional stresses. My questions as to the alleged assault might have led the Committee to ask Ms. Noel about the testimony of Ms. Karas, Dr. Uribe, the three physicians and the police detective who had interviewed and/or examined her, the negative laboratory reports and other data that indicated that no assault had occurred—data which the Committee had made no attempt to obtain and therefore had not considered.

Instead, since I was told that I had only half an hour "for my defense," I, even more succinctly than in the previous meeting, merely reviewed events before and after the crucial morning of September 21, 1984, and then offered to answer any remaining questions by the Committee.

The ensuing communications were so typical of the Committee's confrontational polemics and so reminiscent of the Court of Cards in *Alice in Wonderland* ("Verdict first; evidence, if any, later") that I here paraphrase recorded questions and answers as follows:

By a Freudian analyst

Why, as a trained psychoanalyst, had I not confined my therapy to classical free associations, dream analysis and transference interpretations?

Reply: Freud himself had warned that the pure gold of psychoanalysis had to be alloyed with medical, suggestive and other techniques in the treatment of ego-unstable individuals, as in the therapy of Bruno Walther, Victor Tausk and other of Freud's patients. Incidentally, Freud also admitted that his patients' descriptions of sexual seductions during childhood or later were often wishful fantasies rather than facts.

On neuropharmacology

Some members of the Committee revealed attitudes that were manifestly adversarial, when not frankly prejudicial and derogatory. As but one example of the latter, the following series of questions is quoted verbatim from the legally notarized transcript of the hearing; the inquisitor is necessarily identified for cogency (Transcript pp. 141-143):

By Stuart Yudofsky

Q. Your wife maintains that you are a great scientist, disciplined and dedicated, you must be aware of the neuropsychiatric aspect of the HIV infection, there are literally hundreds of papers on it.

Now may I ask you something else?

Do you agree she [Ms. Noel] had performance anxiety?

Q. What is the documentation that amytal interviews help performance anxiety?

Q. Are you aware of any other biologic treatment for performance anxiety?

Q. It seems as if you're avoiding the published literature on this whole area. There must be a thousand papers related to performance anxiety and biologic interventions, and that very few related to amytal interviews, if any, carefully studied.

Reply: Ms. Noel's anxieties far transcended her occasional difficulties as a nightclub singer. Because of her tendencies to addiction I confined oral medications to Antabuse and dietary vitamins as a preventive or corrective of her alcoholism, and employed amytal in controlled minimal doses, rarely and only for severe stress reactions. This also avoided the serious side effects of Propanolol or Xanax if taken with alcohol.

After numerous other similar interrogations, Christine was permitted to speak briefly, and did so eloquently in my behalf. The hearing then ended with no indication that there would be further sessions.

Outcome: Shortly thereafter I was informed by certified mail that the Illinois Psychiatric Society—an organization I had helped found and of which I had been president—had suspended my membership for five years.

Aside from the technical invalidity of the Committee's procedures, the verdict was in itself anomalous: If I had indeed sexually assaulted Ms. Noel, it was mandatory by IPS regulations that I be expelled rather than merely suspended from the Society and from the American Psychiatric Association (APA). But since the Committee could not find that I had committed any "assault," but had instead inferred that I may have deviated from some standard "pattern of treatment," then the Committee should have awaited, but not pejoratively sought to elicit, such complaints and, if any were received, then considered their validity.

How then to contest the IPS sentence?

The APA. As successively secretary, vice-president and president of the APA I had participated in many top-level sessions in which the verdicts of District Branch Ethics Committees had been routinely labeled "approved" without further review. However, I now felt outraged by cumulative injustices and therefore, on principle, I protested to the national APA Ethics Appeals Board in Washington.

At its hearing on October 6, 1991, Dr. Langsley, who represented the IPS, testified to the Board in a session from which I was excluded; nor was I ever provided with a copy of his dissertation or of the IPS report to the national organization.

Unprepared, therefore, for any formal rebuttals, I again limited my presentation to a review and attested documentation of the facts outlined in Chapter 1, with Dr. Langsley present and silent. We were both then dismissed, giving me an opportunity to tell Dr. Langsley in private precisely what I thought of him with regard to his conduct of the IPS Ethics Committee. (For Christine's opinion, see Chapter 5.)

Follow-up: A few days later the secretary of the APA informed me that, since the IPS Committee had followed its local routine and since there could be no independent investigation, its report would be approved; however, possibly because in the hearings in Washington I had raised doubts as to some of the biased procedures of the IPS Committee, I was assured by then APA President Hartmann that there would be no publicity about my suspension.[Appendix, Reference 7] In effect, I continued to receive invitations to participate in all activities and privileges as a Life Trustee of the APA.

The American Medical Association took a more positive position. After my fiftieth year of membership, on May 23, 1988, the AMA informed me that:

> We are pleased to notify you that at a recent meeting of the Board of Trustees of the Illinois State Medical Society, you were elected to Retired Membership status. We enclose a membership card indicating your new status.
>
> In accord with the provisions of the By-Laws, you will receive all the rights and privileges of membership which you have received in the past.
>
> Sincerely,
> (signed) Boyd E. McCracken, M.D.

Nevertheless, this brief interim of relative tranquillity was also soon to be shattered.

Chapter 4

Book of Job

Early in 1992 I received telephone calls and letters from a Ms. Kathryn Watterson informing me that she was co-authoring a book with Barbara Noel (because, as she explained, Ms. Noel can't write) about Ms. Noel's claim that she had been sexually abused while in therapy with me. The manuscript was virtually complete, but Ms. Watterson nevertheless requested an interview with me for revisions or additions. With the hope of supplying, however late, some truth about the case, I agreed and set a mutually convenient time on the afternoon of April 15. Ms. Watterson came to my home with a male companion whom she introduced as a friend who was to participate in the interview and "take notes." I declined this arrangement in favor of an audiotaped record and the presence of my wife as a concerned witness. Ms. Watterson consented and she, Christine and I conferred in my home library for about two hours.

During the interview I continued to apply my principle of confidentiality and therefore, in response to Ms. Watterson's questions, did not reveal any of Ms. Noel's accounts of her social, sexual, marital and career difficulties; nor would I offer any comments about her motivations or "diagnoses." Instead, I confined the interview to a review of factual and attested material relevant to the credibility of Ms. Noel's allegations, and displayed only such documents as had also been available to her. As to Ms. Watterson's particular concern with the amytal sessions, I showed her descriptions of this therapeutic technique in several psychiatric textbooks including my own, and clarified the supplementary utilization of amytal interviews as especially helpful in Ms. Noel's treatment. All descriptions emphasized that sodium amytal is not an anesthetic and does not render the patient "unconscious"; rather, at an intravenous dose of less than 0.25 gm. it is a mild relaxant, which diminishes anxiety while keeping the patient communicative for sufficient time for a therapeutic interview. (Appendix, Reference 1)

As condensed from the audiotape, but still in adequate detail to be of interest to the readers of this book, some of whom might benefit from the procedures, my explanation was as follows:

In most of Ms. Noel's years of treatment, amytal sessions were unnecessary and were not employed; however, they were occasionally required during the excessively stressful marital, sexual and other crises of 1983 and 1984. When necessary, I then employed mild amytal sedation during interviews designed to alleviate severe depressions and panics and avert self-destructive conduct.

Before Ms. Noel's first amytal session for the relief of a severe life crisis in 1970, she had been given full explanations as to the purpose of the procedure, namely, to diminish tensions and facilitate communication about current stresses and anxieties so that effective means of resolving them could be more clearly considered. She had also, as requested, read the section on Amytal Relaxation in one or more standard psychiatric textbooks in my office, and her remaining questions had been fully answered before she signed a standard "Informed Consent" for the procedure. As with other patients, Ms. Noel was always given the option of having my then secretary, Ms. Savilla Laird, who was also a qualified psychiatric nurse, present throughout the interview, but after her initial experiences she had declined this in preference for complete confidentiality.

The first amytal session was therapeutically effective and Ms. Noel responded well to other modes of treatment so amytal was subsequently used on the average of only once every two or three years.

On the morning of September 21, 1984, I discussed Ms. Noel's presenting problem with her, after which, in accord with the standard routine, she had reclined on a cot in my neurological examining room, rolled her sleeve to the left elbow [contrary to statements in Ms. Watterson's book, no other directives regarding clothing had ever been given her], and received a slow and almost painless intravenous injection of 0.20 gm. of sodium amytal in sterile solution, while I monitored her pulse and blood pressure, and conversed with her for about thirty minutes to elicit and analyze her current difficulties. I correlated the preliminary and amytal interviews for optimal therapeutic effect, offered relevant counsel and received Ms. Noel's expressions of understanding, relief and appreciation. I then left Ms. Noel resting comfortably under the directed care of my office nurse, Ms. Karas, and departed for appointments at Northwestern University. I contrasted this *factual* account, as confirmed by Ms. Karas and others, with Ms. Noel's subsequent allegations and fantasies, to document the falsity of her accusations.

With this prime topic presumably covered, Ms. Watterson requested my evaluations of prominent psychiatrists and other public figures, my comments on medical discoveries, etc. I declined all such invitations for ex-cathedra pronouncements, except to state my hope that, in reporting events of significant current interest, all our media of communication—newspapers, radio, television and especially books with continued readership—would do so in an unbiased, informative and equable manner for balanced public judgments. Ms. Watterson thanked me, promised that her own book "would be fair," summoned her companion from my soundproof music room and departed with professed cordiality.

Follow-up: In the September, 1992, issue of *McCall's* Magazine an article entitled "Broken Trust—A Doctor's Treachery" by Barbara Noel and Kathryn Watterson recounted in sensational detail Ms. Noel's version of her "sexual attack" eight years previously. The account is luridly elaborated by misstatements, distortions, perverse nuances and outright untruths about her "rape" and subsequent experiences—with no mention of the contrary evidence I had presented to Ms. Watterson at her request four months previously. Sufficiently incensed, I wrote a letter of protest to the editor of *McCall's*, and sent an article that briefly presented the attested facts in re the Noel case and Ms. Watterson's interview. The article was rejected, but three months later a version of my letter appeared, condensed but not so edited as to blunt its import.

In early September a book, more accurately entitled *You Must Be Dreaming* in flaming letters, appeared in bookstore windows. This contained even more fantastically prurient details of the "rape"—for instance, that Ms. Noel had detected odors of an after-shave lotion (which I never use) on her body; that I had exposed my "deeply tanned back" (being hypersensitive I avoid all solar damage); that I had the effrontery to invite her to lunch after the "assault" (see my nurse-secretary's sworn testimony in Chapter 1 above proving this to be either a deliberate prevarication or but another of Ms. Noel's wishful "hallucinations" as she herself had described to her examining physicians)—and also included allegations of my involvements with other patients. The chapter entitled "Notes and Sources" featured grossly erroneous versions of my biography (as one example, I had never "collaborated" with my revered mentor,

Adolf Meyer, in determining "the functions of the hypothalamus"), other absurd misinterpretations of my researches on the origins of human behavior, and further distortions of my medical, psychiatric and philosophic teachings. The last chapter, "Afterword: An Interview with Jules Masserman" was equally full of misinformation. For example, my wife (at age seventy-four, a petite 5'3") is described as towering over me (I am 5'8"); conversely, for Ms. Watterson's purposes, I am characterized as "graceful" and "charming" (sexually seductive at age eighty-seven?); whereas, in fact, I have seriously impaired hearing, vision and mobility, and am best described as wizened. Her report of our interview is similarly misleading in that she frequently misquoted me, had not adequately examined the documents I had exhibited, e.g., Nurse Karas' sworn statement, attested refutation of Ms. Noel's claims that she had been subjected to amytal "three times a week!", Detective Kelly's report that he had found no basis for action against me, and other factual data that directly contradicted Ms. Noel's assertions.

Instead, Ms. Watterson blatantly repeated Ms. Noel's bizarre claim that I "had taken [her] to Paris"; whereas I had showed Ms. Watterson evidence that, without my knowledge, Ms. Noel had joined four other patients (a married couple and a mother and daughter) on a publicly advertised excursion to France at a time when I was scheduled to preside at a World Congress of Social Psychiatry at the University of Paris, where I saw her only as part of the group when they attended Congress functions. These examples are merely representative; perceptive readers will discern many inconsistencies, exaggerations, self-contradictions, manifest untruths and other travesties of responsible reporting throughout *You Must Be Dreaming*.

Aftermath. But some readers were not thus perceptive. Christine and I began receiving obscene and/or threatening telephone calls frequently enough to justify having the police monitor our phone line. Peculiarly distressing were requests from newspaper and magazine reviewers for "brief comments" on *You Must Be Dreaming,* whereas to be substantial and valid such "brief comments" could hardly be encompassed in the present volume. So also were the insistent invitations to appear *with* Ms. Noel on national radio and television "talk shows" to which I replied that, whereas I had participated in many educational programs of constructive scientific and social interest, I could not participate in one about an event that, as Ms. Noel herself first admitted, had never happened, and that therefore I could not join her in advertising her book. One such bid from a TV anchorman was phrased in such a way as to confirm that to him "to anchor" meant to be immobilized in mud.

Especially disillusioning when *You Must Be Dreaming* appeared was its high-pitched endorsement by Ann Landers, a syndicated columnist who dispenses advice, mainly on sexual and marital problems, in daily columns printed in newspapers throughout the country. Expanding this role, Ms. Landers had contributed to the blazing orange and navy jacket of the book an arresting kudo: "This shocking documentary, beautifully written, is guaranteed to keep you riveted." Not content with this promotion, on September 13, 1992, Ms. Landers published her own review of the book in an unusually long column, for her (self-estimated) ninety million readers. It began with the darkly anticonspiratorial headline "The Masserman Affair [is] In the Open At Last" and ended with an explicit commercial: "The publisher, Poseidon Press. The price, $21. You will not be able to put it down."

This recalled several curious circumstances in "Ms. Landers'" career. Some years ago when I was an officer and then president of the APA, my wife and I would accept invitations to visit "Ann Landers" (in her identity as Mrs. Eppie Lederer) at her posh Lake Shore Drive apartment looking north over Lake Michigan. There we would, along with other topics, discuss the articles she had asked me to write for her *The Ann Landers Encyclopedia, A to Z.* When published, she had sent me a copy autographed in a large flowing hand:[Appendix, Reference 8]

> For Jules
> With warm thanks and much affection—
> Eppie to you
> Ann Landers to others

and a letter:

> Dear Jules:
> Thanks for that marvelous letter of October 26 and the article on the ingrown toenail. Whimsical it is! Brilliant you are! Delighted I am that we are friends.
> Warm regards,
> Eppie

Although other obligations began to occupy my time, I nevertheless kept track of the career of my erstwhile "friend" and was thereby saddened to hear, among other disconcerting developments:

That she and her first husband had been divorced and that she was having serious difficulties with their daughter Margo

That she had been detected plagiarizing her columns by reprinting items verbatim without acknowledging their previous publication—a transgression for which she had apologized by admitting her literary irresponsibility

That she had advised her readers to seek treatment only from psychologists, because of the danger of sexual seduction by psychiatrists—an oracular directive for which she later apologized on the grounds of absentmindedness

That without permission and without so labeling it, she had incorporated her own language and ideas in a signed letter from a reader, much to the embarrassment of the letter writer and the writer's employer.

But I still could not understand why she was so interested in the Noel case until a friend sent me a clipping from the *New York Times* of September 16, 1992: In sequence, it traced the Noel-Watterson book from an illiterate manuscript submitted by Ms. Noel to Ann Landers, who passed it on to her daughter Margo, whose literary agent recruited Ms. Watterson to write the book and arranged its publication. The *Times* article implied that all are profiting handsomely with Ms. Landers as broker for the enterprise.

The unjust and perfidious publicity engendered by the *McCall's* article, the Watterson book, the TV shows and Ann Landers now required some statement from me to my family, friends and colleagues. I therefore wrote them, with inclusions as to the attested facts of the Noel case, as in Chapter 1 of this book.

I also felt obligated as a Life Trustee of the American Psychiatric Association to write the following letter to Joseph T. English, newly elected president of the APA, with a copy to Melvin Sabshin, its medical director:

Dear Dr. English:

After fifty years of dedicated psychiatric and psychoanalytic practice... I was deeply distressed eight years ago by... charges of a sexual assault by an alcoholic, emotionally unstable woman patient whom I had helped survive severe marital, drug and occupational crises over a period of eighteen years....

Now, at age 87, this distress is renewed by an article in *McCall's* Magazine excerpted from a forthcoming book that fantastically elaborates that patient's allegations....

In justice to myself, as well as the APA, I therefore enclose copies of (1) a letter of protest to *McCall's* and (2) an article reviewing documented evidence that the accusations are completely false.... I trust you will use these communications to the best interests of the APA, an organization I have also

served faithfully and honorably for over fifty years....
  (signed) Jules Masserman
  cc Dr. Melvin Sabshin
  Medical Director, APA
  Enclosures: Attested documents

I received no reply to either letter until after *You Must Be Dreaming* was published and Ann Landers entered the fray. Then, Dr. English's response was devastatingly incendiary: With no notice to me, he had apparently felt it imperative to hold a closed meeting of the Board of Trustees. The Board, not recognizing that Ms. Landers' tirade against me, as a past president of the APA and four other psychiatric societies, was but another instance of her oft expressed hostility to psychiatrists and psychiatry in general, and seemingly fearing another more overt public expression of antagonism to psychiatry, had presumably authorized Dr. English to send her a craven letter of apology, and to publish a statement in the APA *Psychiatric News* of October 16, 1992, to the effect that the Board was "outraged that Jules Masserman had repeatedly [sic] drugged and raped patients"*—thus ceding to Ms. Landers another public triumph over the APA and psychiatry, diminishing her concern that some daring psychiatrist might comment on her often amateurish and counterproductive advice to her readers—and incidentally encouraging more of them to prefer false charges against members of the APA in the hope of sharing in the advertised profits of those who do so.

In a succession of executive positions in the APA I had collaborated with many fellow Trustees in averting self-injurious APA decisions and actions. After half a century of devotion and

---

* Nonetheless, on January 29th, 1993, Dr. Melvin Sabshin, Medical Director, wrote to thank me for 57 years of continued "guidance of the APA"(Appendix, Reference 9) and, apparently on second thought, Dr. English had shortly before urged me as an APA Fellow and Trustee in good standing, to extend my services also to the World Federation for Mental Health.

honored contributions to psychiatry I trust that more perceptive, thoughtful and just leaders will again emerge to serve the
APA's best scientific and organizational interests, and restore
the dignity and probity of a discipline that should rank high
among the humanistic studies and services.

The Minor Key. I thought that by this time, with the aid of
Christine, the support of many true friends and with interim
accomplishments (articles, books and songs published), I had
become fairly inured to disappointments and injustices, but I
admit that the APA's action once again deeply disillusioned me
about fair-weather colleagues. Result: an interim recurrence of
insomnia, anorexia, loss of weight, energy and creativity and—
truth be told—even depressive ruminations that perhaps life
was now hardly worth living—thoughts almost instantly dismissed by considerations for Christine's welfare.

Fortunately these preoccupations were relatively transient
and my quasi-paranoid extensions were further mitigated by
newspaper and magazine articles questioning Ms. Noel's and
Ms. Landers' credibility, by prospective authors who wished
"to write books about famous men unjustly accused and tor-
mented" (presenting me as a current instance), and by television shows that turned in my favor. One example of the latter
was the videotaped session in our home, where CNBC's
Michelle Avny interviewed Christine and me intelligently and
empathetically for about an hour for subsequent broadcast on
a series entitled "The Real Story."

We did not wait to view this broadcast; instead, we flew to
India, where I presided at the Thirteenth World Congress of
Social Psychiatry in Delhi. There, as a delightful surprise, the
Congress celebrated the fiftieth year of Christine's and my mar-
riage (i.e., we had seen a thousand full moons) by staging an
elaborate Hindu Wedding Ceremony in a moonlit garden.
Accordingly, I was provided with a golden turban and breast-

plate for me, and gold ornaments, a richly jeweled headdress, veil and bridal sari for Christine—after which we were sanctified by reciting Vedic verses around a sacred fire in an improvised temple to Brahma, Siva and especially Vishnu and his gentle current consort Sitka, deities of peace and creativity. Thus blessed, we embarked on a second honeymoon cruise from Bombay to Indonesia on the gracefully seaworthy, luxurious motor yacht appropriately named Renaissance VII, for a visit to Singapore, a prearranged overnight at Phuket to conduct a seminar aboard ship with a delegation of Thai psychiatrists from Bangkok, a pause next day near erupting Krakatau for scenery, dust and fumes, en route to Komodo for a strenuous trek to its overadvertised "dragons," and on to Bali for a mountain climb to honor its Mother Temple where all Hindu sects are welcome to pray peacefully together—although still only once a year.

Our renewed appreciation of the world's beauties, benefits and bounties was hardly affected on our return home by a routine inquiry from the Chicago Psychoanalytic Society as to my plans. I affirmed my retirement, and we proceeded to decorate our home for the holidays, including our traditional tree. Among the most harmonious of these decorations were scores of cards and letters from colleagues, former students or patients and many other friends expressing continued esteem, support and warm personal friendship.

Thus ended the reverse-banner year of 1992.

Chapter 5

Familial Travails

Christine McGuire Masserman

Like the families of the seventeenth century Salem women tragically condemned to exile or hanging as witches, and like all those before and since whose loved ones have been the innocent victims of the mistakes, hallucinations, mental disturbances, mass delusions, greed or viciousness of others—I, too, for almost a decade, have shared the suffering inflicted on my husband *for something that never happened!*

As anyone who has experienced it can testify, in such situations the most difficult and painful burden for the family is having to stand by helplessly while a cherished member is being cruelly, callously, repeatedly hurt, and being unable to do anything to stop his persecution. Smelling blood drawn by the carnage of the initial charge, scavenging accusers, greedy attorneys and salacious media gather for the kill and, most disgusting of all, ambitious prosecutors and pandering colleagues join in. Like a pack of wild dogs nipping at the heels of an injured creature, they try—with all too frequent success—to bring down with a thousand wounds, even the most majestic prey. While that may be the inescapable law of the jungle, it should not be allowed to govern a presumably civilized society.

In even marginally dysfunctional families such stress soon becomes too great and the family is literally torn apart. But in those who are bound together by deep mutual respect and affection, and whose members have genuinely shared each other's joys and sorrows, the travails that follow false accusations may actually bring them even closer together. And so it has been for Jules and me—we have found a new intimacy that has been one of our prime sources of happiness amidst the intense passions aroused by the travesty we have suffered.

And so, as the days and, now, years of unjust harassment continued, I have felt—along with the intermittent sense of unreality and disbelief that this could be happening to respectable and respected people such as ourselves who have always lived by the rules—ever greater love for the thoroughly decent and dedicated man being subjected to unceasing attacks. For their perpetrators and the venal attorneys and journalists who encourage such behavior for their own profit, I continue to feel anger, indignation and at times outright hatred.

For a system that condones, facilitates and even rewards such despicable conduct I can feel only outrage, along with intense frustration and occasional despair at being unable to get the truth out. In contrast, the enduring friendships and the understanding and support we continue to receive from so many people, friends and strangers alike, has brought us unalloyed joy. And throughout this seemingly unending ordeal I have held two abiding convictions: deep pride in the strength and dignity with which Jules has unfailingly conducted himself in the face of vicious and unrelenting injustice, and utter contempt for the few hypocritical and unprincipled officers of one psychiatric organization who, in craven capitulation to the demonstrably false allegations against Jules made by an obviously disturbed and admittedly delusional patient, publicly denounced him—a man widely regarded as one of the organization's most honored living members.

I was brought up to condemn such behavior and to believe that honesty, decency and loyalty would inspire similar responses from others. And so while I may someday be able to understand and perhaps even to forgive the patient whose especially vivid dream initiated our decade-long nightmare, I can feel only revulsion for those few colleagues whose cowardly condemnation of my husband has come near to destroying my valued illusions and has forced me, however reluctantly, to be wary of some of my fellow man. Fortunately, this unwelcome vigilance extends only to the transient factotums who wield their petty privileges with such arrogance. With the valued support of many friends, my treasured faith in the essential decency of others still remains basically intact, despite the injustices we have suffered.

My Background

That precious faith was instilled in my childhood home where it was simply taken for granted that everyone should love, support and help everyone else. There was never the slightest doubt that members of my family would share anything we had with each other: from our views about books, plays, art, people, politics, religion and all the other topics that constituted the subjects of our always lively discussions around the family dinner table, to the most cherished possessions we had to give—our time, our labors, our lives. From our earliest days, my younger sister and I both knew we could always depend on our gentle, scholarly parents, whose remarkable partnership was based on their devotion to each other and to us.

This comfortable feeling was reinforced by my childhood experience in the neighborly warmth of a small Southern village on the edge of the Kentucky Bluegrass, only an hour away from the homes of my indulgent grandparents and a host of congenial aunts, uncles and cousins, whose ancestors had come as pioneers to that area in the mid-1700s.

Uprooted by the Great Depression we moved to a "strange land"—the North, where we settled in one of the tiny (population: one thousand) church-dominated towns that dot the Ohio countryside. Both of my parents had obtained positions on the faculty of the small liberal arts college there and, not surprisingly in my view, soon became among its most popular professors. Though we were about the only people in town who had never served at least one missionary term in Africa, we were immediately made to feel welcome. It was a place where everyone knew nearly everyone else in quiet, friendly ways; most attended church regularly and many participated in the educational and other activities of the college. I regarded everyone as a friend and had no doubt that any one of them would come to my assistance should I need it.

I attended the public high school in that protective atmosphere and then went on to the local college, where with the aid of my parents' example (and a then popular Southern accent), I managed to find a place in most of the extracurricular activities, from basketball and ballet to drama and debate. I graduated first in my class at age eighteen, but going out into a world of 20% to 25% unemployment presented more challenge than I wished to take on. I, therefore, gladly accepted the good offices of a family friend who arranged for me to obtain a generous research assistantship that paid all my expenses for three years of graduate study at the prestigious University of Chicago.

I had enjoyed my small town life and had planned to stay in Chicago only long enough to complete my graduate studies, and then to seek out another little college community where I could establish the kind of home in which I had grown up. But when, at age twenty-one, I was offered a position at the university as an Instructor in the Department of Economics—a previously exclusive preserve of elderly males—the combination of temptation and inertia proved too strong to resist.

In the early 1940s the university was engaged in two major projects: one, as I learned later, was the development of nuclear weapons to Win The War; the second, conjoint studies of history, sociology, statesmanship and (13th century Thomistic) philosophy to Win The Peace. Soon after joining the faculty I was invited to participate in interdisciplinary conferences related to Project Two. At one of those I heard Jules, a young Assistant Professor in Psychiatry, present a paper on human behavior, the clarity, wit and cogency of which intrigued me. We met, I accepted his shy invitation to go sailing (see his wry account in Chapter 11) and my life was irrevocably changed. We were married on February 20, 1943, spent our brief honeymoon in a snow-bound country cottage, and returned to find the proofs of his first book dedicated, as have been all his subsequent publications, "To Christine, As Ever." The pattern of sharing that we instinctively adopted in jointly putting the final touches on that manuscript continues, after fifty years, to characterize our life together.

We soon moved into an apartment overlooking Lake Michigan, where we still live, accepted academic advancements (Jules at Northwestern University and I at the University of Illinois at Chicago), pursued our many common interests (tennis, golf, sailing, music, travel), acquired many mutual friends, and were quietly proud of each other's attainments and honors. In general, we led a contented and productive life together for more than forty years until the fateful morning of September 21, 1984, when a fantastic event initiated the series of incredible consequences recounted by Jules in the preceding chapters. It is their devastating effects on our lives that I shall describe, with deep empathy for Jules' suffering, admiration for his fortitude, pride in his integrity and, at times, serious concern for his survival.

Professional Context: Helpers At Risk

Most people recognize the occupational hazards that firemen, policemen, miners and many others face daily, but few are fully aware of the dangers that confront persons in the health professions—particularly physicians, psychologists and other therapists who work with troubled patients and clients, many of whom are deeply depressed, frequently suicidal or aggressively hostile, even homicidal. One of our close friends was fatally shot in his university office by a male patient whose outward calm had deceived even the experienced receptionist. Conversely, patients are often prey to bizarre fantasies about their therapists, and irrational and unwelcome attachments are commonplace. For example, the wife of a colleague was followed for several weeks by a jealous female patient who could be persuaded to desist only after a court order was obtained. In short, in my husband's specialty the helper all too often becomes the victim, blamed by patients, clients and their families for any disappointments.

Knowing of these risks from the experience of friends and colleagues, I was therefore understandably proud that for over forty years Jules had conducted an exemplary practice which had earned him a well-deserved reputation as an outstanding clinician among colleagues who often referred not only some of their more difficult cases to him, but who also frequently sent friends and family members to him for counsel, as did the many patients he had helped.

Of course, Jules had never discussed his patients with me; rather I learned how highly he was regarded directly from them and from his colleagues. At any social or professional gathering, especially in Chicago, some people always came up to me, introduced themselves, said how pleased they were to meet me and launched into an account of how Jules had helped them or their families and friends. For more than forty years I had therefore not only shared in Jules' many attainments as a highly respected physician, teacher, consultant, author and scientist, I had also been the proud recipient of unsolicited testimony from his many patients and colleagues, as to his integrity, his thoughtfulness and his expertise.

And so, though fully aware of the hazards in his field, I was unprepared for the monstrous attack launched against my husband in the fall of 1984 by a middle-aged patient whom he had helped off and on for almost twenty years. I knew that Jules was simply not capable of knowingly doing harm to another human being, except perhaps to protect an endangered life. Nor could I imagine that any rational person would place any credence in Ms. Noel's bizarre tale. After all: How probable is it that an internationally renowned psychiatrist would risk a reputation he had worked a lifetime to earn by assaulting anyone, anywhere? How probable is it that, in the face of the AIDS epidemic, an intelligent physician would endanger his own life by having casual sexual contact with anyone, especially a person he may have had reason to believe had indulged in high risk behaviors? How probable is it that a healthy, middle-aged woman, who was *actually* being raped, would "pretend to be asleep" (as Ms. Noel claimed she had done), and make *no effort* to rid herself of a frail (130 pound), eighty-year-old physician whom she had known to be unfailingly helpful for over eighteen years? How probable is it that *any* woman would fail to call the office nurse or to make *any* effort to summon help, known to be within easy hearing only a few feet away on both sides of her?

The answers to these questions are obvious to any fair-minded person of normal intelligence. But it was difficult to take comfort in Ms. Noel's lack of credibility because I also knew that when sexual misconduct is charged, there is a strong tendency—even covert pressure—in the cynical and turbulent times in which we live, to accept the accuser's story, to reject the accused's denials and the evidence he or she presents, as merely routine and self-serving, and to denigrate support of family and friends as misguided efforts, at best to be pitied.

And so, at the risk of some repetition of my husband's earlier account, here is my view of our travails.

An Unfolding Nightmare

Actually it all began in early July of 1984, when we received word that Miss Laird, who had served loyally as Jules' office nurse for over thirty years, had died of a heart attack at her home. Though we did not realize it at the time, her death heralded a series of events that, in improbable combinations, eventuated in the travesty that soon engulfed us. Had she lived, Miss Laird would have been able, on the basis of her credentials as a psychiatric nurse and her intimate knowledge of Jules' practice and his patients, to provide independent expert testimony about his professional treatment of them and the benefits each had received—evidence that would have done much to discredit the preposterous allegations against him.

I no longer remember the sequence of the other adversities that soon befell us, but over the course of a few days in late September, 1984, we learned that laboratory tests ordered in the course of Jules' annual physical examination were essentially diagnostic of cancer of the prostate, that my by then exceedingly painful back and increasing limitations of activity could not be attributed to simple "muscle strain," and that, after nearly fifty years of blameless and highly satisfactory practice, Jules was being sued for a "sexual assault" on a patient.

The first order of business, even before taking care of our own health, was to report the threatened suit to Jules' insurance company, who replied that a Mr. Kelly, a senior partner in the law firm of Hinshaw, Culbertson, et al., was being retained to represent Jules. Despite Mr. Kelly's reassurances as to the probabilities of a quick and favorable disposition of the suit, I was deeply apprehensive about the entire matter and greatly concerned about its effect on Jules, especially in view of his age (then nearly eighty) and his need for urgent surgery. When after several weeks we had heard nothing more, we tried to contact Mr. Kelly only to be told that his firm was going through a major reorganization, that he and several senior partners had left and that the complaint against Jules was "now being handled" by Ms. Debra Davy, a young associate in the firm.

Though Jules thought we should trust his insurers, I was profoundly troubled by the reassignment of his defense to a junior attorney with limited experience in this highly specialized and extremely sensitive field of litigation. Whatever her demonstrated dedication and intelligence, I was deeply disturbed that Ms. Davy's firm was sending her up alone, against a seasoned team of aggressive personal injury lawyers ready to exploit any possible inexperience or lack of expertise on her part. Even now, almost ten years later, I feel that had Hinshaw, Culbertson et al. assigned an experienced attorney to replace Mr. Kelly, Ms. Noel's case would have been promptly and vigorously contested and that would have been the end of it: there would have been no other suits, no devastating publicity, no derivative complaints to professional associations and licensing agencies, and certainly no sensational and lurid books and TV shows about a transgression *that demonstrably never occurred.*

These alternative outcomes of a competent defense were rendered even more likely by the fact that Ms. Noel's first attorney, after investigating her fantastic complaints, had obtained the Court's permission to withdraw as her advocate and that at least one other equally ethical attorney had refused to represent her. Nevertheless, after much searching Ms. Noel finally found a lawyer who was willing to take her case on a contingency fee basis, and shortly thereafter I learned from Jules that several of his patients were reporting that Ms. Noel had repeatedly attempted to pressure them to join her suit, with bizarre assertions that Jules had also poisoned his former nurse for various evil reasons.

This initiated a period of growing apprehensions and tensions, exacerbated by my feeling that no one was doing anything to counter the dreadful charges against Jules. Not knowing what to expect, I tried during these ever more troubling days to hide my mounting concern from Jules so as not to add to his already heavy burdens, and to help in the only way I knew by redoubling my efforts to make our home a peaceful and pleasant refuge and myself a devoted and outwardly calm helpmate.

After what seemed an interminable period of uncertainty and inaction, Ms. Noel's and the insurance company's attorneys finally began to schedule a series of depositions and conferences. Unfortunately, this was precisely at the time when Jules was hospitalized for urgent surgery. In quick succession in the autumn and early winter of 1984-85 he underwent three operations, each of which required general anesthesia—a scary procedure for any eighty-year-old. In between hospitalizations he was subjected to repeated lengthy inquisitions, previously arranged by telephone calls made directly to his hospital room and scheduled to occur during what were supposed to be quiet periods for recovery. Instead, these interrogations sometimes lasted for several hours during which Jules was grilled by two aggressive trial lawyers whose hostile questions, as recorded in the transcripts, often went far afield in attempts to trick him into making some damaging statement.

I could not believe that this level of harassment could be allowed to continue for months with no objections from the attorney retained by Jules' insurance company presumably to protect his interests, and with no sign of any comparable pressure being placed on his accuser. Nonetheless, searching for some encouraging sign, I became cautiously hopeful, despite all appearances to the contrary, when I learned that arrangements had been made to videotape one of his forthcoming depositions. Assuming that the taping was being done to minimize the strain of future court appearances, I ventured a word of appreciation to Ms. Davy. Her chilling response—"God forbid he should die before I conclude this case," implying that she was merely taking precautions to have a legal record "in case"—served only to exacerbate my worries about Jules' chances for surviving the mounting stresses of the Noel suit.

Meanwhile, he was also preoccupied with worry about me. By early 1985 I was no longer ambulatory, yet with no firm diagnosis or remedy. Deeply concerned about my progressive invalidism, Jules could not monitor the Noel case, much less attempt to direct it to a successful conclusion; instead, he was almost constantly with me during my innumerable medical, X-ray and surgical consultations.

The reader will understand why, under these circumstances, we failed to recognize until it was too late that Jules did not have adequate legal representation of his, as opposed to the insurance company's, interests. The difficulty arises from the fact that the attorney who defends a physician against a malpractice suit is selected, retained and paid by the insurance company, and is therefore under pressure to conclude the litigation in a way most favorable to the insurer, though that may not necessarily be in the best interest of the insured physician, who lacks even normal attorney-client privileges. I believe that had either, or preferably both, of us been reasonably healthy so as to exert effective pressure in shaping the response to the preposterous allegations against Jules, the entire matter would have been quickly put to rest before it exploded out of control.

As I later came to understand, the attorney retained by Jules' insurance firm had, from the very beginning, three options: to enter a prompt motion for dismissal, to begin vigorous "discovery" procedures in preparation for going to trial, or to explore possible settlement arrangements. While no one can predict with certainty what a particular judge or jury will do, in view of the incontrovertible evidence from unbiased witnesses (Ms. Karas, Jules' office nurse, Ms. Noel's internist, her gynecologist, the Emergency Room physicians, the two police investigators, the reports from the crime laboratory, etc.) contradicting Ms. Noel's account, and her own voluntary statements that she may have been "dreaming" and/or "hallucinating," it is highly probable that either of the first two strategies, pursued by an experienced attorney knowledgeable in this field of tort law, would have been successful. One such attorney who specializes in this type of litigation subsequently suggested to me that either tactic could (and probably should) have been combined with a countersuit against Ms. Noel and her attorneys under what my friend called "Rule 11." This is a relatively recent provision in the law that holds plaintiff's attorney personally accountable and legally liable for bringing a "frivolous" or "fraudulent" action and/or for failing to investigate the client's allegations fully.

However, rather than mounting a vigorous counterattack, Ms. Davy chose very early to pursue a settlement agreement. As she explained to us much later, she went that route because she believed that, in view of Jules' prominence in his field, the case would become a "media circus"—played out daily in the papers and on the afternoon TV talk shows and the evening newscasts—over the many weeks and possibly months during which a public trial could drag on. She told us that she feared that under those circumstances an extended trial, with the necessity for possibly lengthy testimony and its potential for unfavorable publicity, would place too much stress on Jules, given his advanced age and his seriously impaired health.

While all that is possibly true, publicly contesting Ms. Noel's unsupported allegations could not have been nearly as bad as the consequences of a "settlement" that settled nothing and that failed in its most elementary purposes of protecting us from the travails we still suffer: escalating public claims by Ms. Noel with no supporting evidence, threatened suits by persons admittedly attracted by the prospect of large financial awards with no risk, consequent public expressions of "outrage" by a professional association which did not trouble to elicit the facts and confirm that there had been *no* "sexual assault" or any other professional transgressions and, indeed, that Ms. Noel's therapy had at least enabled her to function most of the time at a reasonably effective level for almost twenty years.

There are many reasons that innocent victims of false allegations so often suffer such painful consequences of highly publicized out-of-court settlements. Though the law is very clear that settlement of a case does *not* constitute an admission of culpability or liability, most people find it hard to believe that an insurance company will "pay out good money" to settle a case against an innocent client, and so they conclude that the accused is actually guilty. Furthermore, the public generally fails to realize that insurance lawyers normally assume (as did Ms. Davy in 1985) that any reasonable out-of-court settlement is of advantage to the company, since it avoids quickly mounting attorneys' fees and court costs, years of litigation and the possibility, however remote, of an adverse verdict with multi-million dollar awards by an unpredictable judge or jury reflecting currently irrational hostilities to psychiatrists and other physicians. In such a situation, the interests of the insured, however vital, necessarily become secondary to "the business interests" of the insurance firm (as described in Chapter 6).

Nor do most people understand that in cases such as ours, a settlement, whatever its terms, is never between the accuser and the accused; it is between the accuser's lawyers and the *insurer* of the accused. For example, in the settlement by Jules' insurance company, Jules was not involved in any negotiations; he was not a party to the agreement; he did not sign it; and he has never even seen a copy of it. We were notified only by a duplicate note from Ms. Davy to Jules' insurance firm that she had settled Ms. Noel's claim for a shocking $200,000.

Whatever the reasons for that settlement—Ms. Davy's stated concern for Jules' health, respect for the business interests of the insurance company, or some other consideration—it is clear, in retrospect, that the decision not to contest Ms. Noel's charge was disastrous for us, made more so by what, as Ms. Davy later informed us, was only an unwritten "gentlemen's agreement" with Ms. Noel's lawyers that there would be no publicity about the settlement. I am convinced that if it had been clear from the outset that any persons making any allegations against Jules would be required to defend those claims in Court under oath where they would be exposing themselves to cross-examination and to possible prosecution for perjury, we would not have had to endure a decade of tribulation.

Instead, I cannot adequately plumb the depths of disillusionment, resentment and victimization that Jules and I felt—reactions to recur with sometimes insufferable intensities during the mounting publicity and growing injustices the Noel "settlement" initiated. Without prior warning, Jules received a letter from his insurance company that because of the settlement *it* had negotiated, it was canceling his professional liability insurance, effective immediately. Though Jules had already taken steps to initiate his long anticipated retirement, he now had to choose between the equally unpleasant alternatives of abruptly canceling his commitments to patients under his care or completing his obligations without any liability coverage. As the honorable man he has always been, he accepted the risks and chose the latter course.

The next fallout from Ms. Davy's vaunted settlement and spurious "gentlemen's agreement" was in many ways even more unsettling: a sensationally headlined and luridly worded article in the *Chicago Tribune* (January 6, 1987) proclaiming that Jules, "the most prominent psychiatrist in the world," had drugged and sexually assaulted an unspecified number of female patients, and had settled the claim of one of them, "a singer-actress," for $200,000. To assist others who might wish to obtain similar prizes just on the basis of "[their i.e., the patient's] word versus the word of the doctor," the names and institutional affiliation of Ms. Noel's attorneys were conveniently supplied.

Professional Justice:
Public Agencies—Private Monitors

That article understandably provoked investigations by the Illinois Department of Professional Regulation (IDPR), the official state agency that issues licenses to physicians and other professionals. This time Jules promptly hired his own attorney, one recommended to him as expert in dealing with the IDPR. There followed another year of one painful trauma after another—relieved only by a totally unrelated event, surgical intervention that produced my miraculous recovery of pain-free mobility after two and one half years of disability.

Meanwhile, the macabre ballet between the IDPR and the attorney we had retained played out according to its own prescribed script. Jules' lawyer advised him that, in view of the evidence, it seemed reasonable to conclude that Ms. Noel and any other complainants "could easily be impeached," and that contesting their allegations before the IDPR would present an opportunity for Jules to establish his innocence. But, as we considered our options, it became evident that Jules' only choice was between implementing his planned retirement as soon as he had completed the treatment of his remaining patients, or engaging in stressful, expensive, lengthy, public hearings only for the dubious privilege of continuing to keep open a medical practice which he had already arranged to close. We discussed this choice and, in view of many considerations, including especially our long anticipated post-retirement plans (management of the Masserman Foundation for International Accords, overseas lecture commitments, projected writing and travel), we opted to proceed with retirement as previously arranged, *provided* Jules' attorney could reach a reasonable understanding with IDPR that such a course of action implied *no* culpability. That was arranged and once again we dared to hope that our troubles had ended.

Once again, however, fate decreed otherwise. Literally within a few days of signing the accord with IDPR and only thirty-six hours before our scheduled departure for an invitational lecture tour of Australia and New Zealand, another outrageous story appeared in the *Tribune,* this time about Jules' agreement with IDPR, implying that there was something sinister about his decision to retire at age eighty-four (!) and hinting that it was tantamount to an admission of guilt for some unspecified transgressions, thus once again triggering letters and recorded calls to be ignored or answered on our return.

Even in the absence of such unjust sequelae as we continued to suffer, there is, for those falsely accused, a profoundly frustrating aspect to all highly publicized settlements and agreements: namely, the charges are given wide circulation but the accused rarely has any opportunity to counteract them and "to set the record straight." And so, painful as it was to contemplate reliving our ordeal, Jules and I tried to take a positive view of the summons he received in the autumn of 1989 to appear at a special meeting of the Ethics Committee of the Illinois Psychiatric Society (IPS) to answer Ms. Noel's preposterous complaint that he had "drugged" and "raped" her five years previously. We hoped that the occasion would, at least, provide an opportunity for him to vindicate himself in what we trustingly believed would be an objective hearing before an impartial jury of his peers and, thereby, give us a chance to exorcise the demons that had haunted us for five long years.

But our trust was sadly misplaced. As Jules has described in Chapter 3 and the Committee's official minutes explicitly confirm, under the chairmanship of Donald Langsley, the Committee repeatedly sought to obtain damaging statements of dubious veracity from women whom Ms. Noel had solicited to join her suit for monetary gain and who admittedly knew nothing about the only issue legitimately before the Committee—namely, the events that took place in Jules' office on the morning of September 21, 1984. The minutes also make clear that the Committee had made no effort at any time to contact the many reputable, independent and knowledgeable persons who had interviewed and/or examined Ms. Noel on the day of the alleged attack.

When I realized the extent of the Committee's commitment to the *prosecution*, rather than to the objective *investigation* and *adjudication* of the charge against Jules, I could no longer refrain from writing to the chairman, pointing out in detail the Committee's flagrant and repeated violations of even its own minimal procedural requirements (with respect to duration, impartiality and comprehensiveness of the investigation, opportunity for defense, etc.) designed to provide some measure of protection of the rights of innocent victims of false accusations. I concluded my letter (here paraphrased for brevity) as follows:

> I understand and respect the importance of the Committee's responsibilities to protect the public from unethical, incompetent or impaired practitioners. But surely the Committee has an *equal and reciprocal responsibility* to

protect the legitimate rights of members when these are violated by unsupported allegations of seriously disturbed and/or greedy patients.

In the hope that justice may yet prevail, I trust that your Committee will correct its defalcations and try to understand what has actually happened over the past five years and why it has happened. I ask only that *you not blame Jules for my action* in the event you find anything I have said to be offensive.

Nothing can erase the anxieties and depressions we have suffered as a consequence of the false allegations against Jules, but I remain proud of the strength and dignity he has shown. For five long years he has tried to avoid burdening family and friends with his own troubles and sorrow, and he has courageously persisted in fulfilling his lecture commitments at home and abroad, in completing his writing (two new books published in 1989 and a third contracted for 1990), and in implementing a variety of initiatives to bring better understanding among peoples across the globe. I don't know how anybody can take the injustice Jules has suffered and still go on behaving like the decent and caring person he has never ceased to be. But, Don, I do know that everyone, no matter how strong, has a breaking point; what I do not know is how close we are to ours.

Under the circumstances, I do not see how the cause of justice can possibly be served by the unjust prosecution of an 85-year-old, demonstrably innocent, world renowned, retired physician. I ask only for a fair and unbiased hearing so that Jules may be given a chance to present the incontrovertible evidence of his innocence and that we may then be allowed to live out whatever time we have left together, in the peace and serenity we have surely earned by a lifetime of service.

Follow-up: My sincerely friendly and heartfelt letter did no good. The Committee persisted not only in acting as prosecutor, judge and jury, but also in violating all semblance of fair procedure, minimal evidentiary standards and even the basic requirements of due process laid down by its parent organization.

I was so antagonized by the hypocrisy of our "old friend" that when, after the Committee's second hearing, Dr. Langsley notified Jules of its (his?) decision, I sent a second missive to "Dear Don" in which I more candidly appraised his character as witnessed by his reputed arrogance, insensitivity and disregard for the rights of others, especially evident in his recent misdirection of the IPS Ethics Committee. Here are a few publishable excerpts:

> Had you really believed Jules guilty of rape, the only complaint to the IPS of which he has ever been informed, you should have fought to have him expelled and/or to have him treated like any other "impaired" physician required to enter appropriate therapy; that was your obligation as a human being, a physician and an officer of the Society. If he was *not* guilty of rape, and *the IPS Committee minutes clearly state that [there was no such finding],* then you should have fought to prevent any censure. [The Committee's records reveal that this was] recommended because some members...disagreed with Jules' [comprehensive] mode of treatment....[If so], then the whole procedure was illegal since there had been no complaint on that score, and it was your duty to so [inform] the APA....The Committee had no right to draft its own complaint [or to have its agents seek new plaintiffs]...and try to pressure them into making additional charges.
>
> In any case, under your chairmanship the entire IPS proceedings were unethically and illegally persecutorial. In the interest of justice you had a duty, at the very least, to [consult] with the many reliable informants who had independent, objective evidence relevant to the incredibility of Barbara Noel's sole complaint: [Eight persons were then listed with a brief summary of the attested evidence available from each.] Why did IPS never contact any of these people?
>
> With all due affection,
> (signed) Christine Masserman

P.S. Jules has not seen this letter; it is a statement of how I feel. Don't blame him.

Though I realize that such a letter will hardly transform a man of Langsley's character, I doubt that I, at least, will ever again have to endure his particularly odious form of "sexual harassment," which for years consisted, every time he saw me, of waddling across a room with arms outstretched, yelling "Hello, Dear Heart" —and then planting a wet, slobbery kiss on my reluctant cheek.

Continuing Organizational Perfidy

But sexual aggression in the reverse sense of harassment of the innocent was not yet to abate. When, despite assurances from then President Hartmann that there would be no publicity, [Appendix, Reference 7] an especially vicious tirade appeared in the official newsletter of the APA, Jules wrote the editor, Robert Campbell, as follows: "If there is still justice and decency in the APA, you will publish this long but cogent letter [summarizing the attested facts] about the Noel episode." His letter remains unacknowledged and unpublished.

And a year after the IPS-APA experience, Jules was requested to respond to a review of the Noel-Watterson book that appeared in the *Psychiatric Times*. The review had been written by Alan Stone, Jules' successor as president of the APA. Jules replied as follows:

To the Editor:

I appreciate Alan Stone's accolades, but deeply regret that he did not follow his juristic training to ascertain the truth about the Noel book before writing his grossly misleading review. As requested by Michael Grinfeld, Associate Editor of the *Times*, and necessarily condensed, the facts are these:

Ms. Noel was my patient for eighteen years, during which time she repeatedly expressed her gratitude for my help in resolving life crises I cannot ethically describe. However, on the morning of September 21, 1984, while mildly sedated for a severe panic-depressive state, she apparently had a vividly wishful sexual fantasy. She did not complain to me or to my office nurse, who later testified under oath that she had been present throughout the morning, had routinely checked on Ms. Noel twice while she rested after I had left the office for appointments at my University, and that on both occasions had found her resting comfortably, fully alert and pleasantly communicative.

Ms. Noel nevertheless immediately consulted her internist, then her gynecologist, then a University Emergency Room physician. To all she volunteered that she may have "dreamed" or "hallucinated" a rape; clarifying this, their ensuing physical, vaginal and extensive forensic laboratory findings showed no evidence of any assault. Two police detectives, after their own inquiries and reviews of the data, reported to the Crime Division that "victim stated she was unable to determine whether incident was a dream or reality," and they "request[ed] that case be EX-CLEARED," i.e., no charges justified.

Still persistent, Ms. Noel consulted a prominent Chicago attorney who, after an independent survey declined to take her case, as did a similarly ethical female counselor. However, Ms. Noel finally engaged a lawyer to file a civil suit for "physical assault," on a contingency fee basis and, whether or not so advised, she began canvassing my female patients to join her litigation, informing them, among other charges, that I was also a drug addict and had poisoned my previous office nurse, who had been my secretary for 32 years. She found only two (both with delinquent accounts) to share her expected awards; one was a lawyer who, after completing successful therapy two years previously had invited Mrs. Masserman and myself as distinguished guests of honor at her wedding; the other was her bridesmaid, whose letters of gratitude for her two years of treatment I also have on file. Both had apologized for accounts overdue.

At this point, the attorney for my insurance firm proposed that, in view of my age (82), debilitating illnesses (three surgical interventions), and my wife's concurrent arthritic invalidism, it would be best to avoid years of stressful litigation by settling Ms. Noel's suit out of court, on terms of complete confidentiality and no admission of any culpability. I considered this but signed no formal consent and was not consulted further; instead, I was informed of the settlement only after it was concluded and, to my horror, widely publicized—the probable source of Dr. Stone's "rumors" of my misbehavior.

Two years later, on Ms. Noel's complaint, another "investigation" (during which not one of the reputable and favorable witnesses designated above was contacted) was made by the Illinois Psychiatric Society Ethics Committee, which concluded that they differed with my integrated analytic-pharmacologic-behavioral modes of therapy of Ms. Noel, but could find no evidence of any sexual transgression—hence the verdict of "suspension," but not "expulsion."

When Dr. Stone's review of the nine-year-old episode was brought to my attention by indignant colleagues, I sent my erstwhile friend a letter with the salutation "Et tu Brute?" and a summary of legally attested data confirming all the statements in this letter. I have received no reply, but I suppose I should be grateful for his decision to render his final verdict when my "suspension" terminates five years hence. Since I am now in my eighty-ninth year, this presumably expresses his kind wish for my longevity.

During a lifetime dedicated to psychiatric research, writing and half a century of lauded practice I have received incredible honors and, more important, acquired worldwide friendships and loyalties. I can spare Dr. Stone's and that of others who, ignoring contrary data, recently branded a colleague on illusory allegations alone. "Verdict first, evidence later"—Alan in Wonderland.

Deep appreciation to the *Psychiatric Times* for its editorial probity.

(Signed) Jules H. Masserman, M.D.

In contrast, a past-president of an APA District Branch wrote Jules feelingly, as follows:

"I must say Ms. Noel's description of your behavior doesn't jibe with anything I know about you. Her book [with Ms. Watterson] shows obvious evidence of [a diagnosis] that would be clear to even a first year resident....To not vigorously defend someone of your status, not to speak of undisputed good character will cost the APA far more in the long run....When our ethics committees [ignore the] evidence, we are all doomed to lives of assured terror."

Unfortunately, it is often "politically correct" for an "Establishment" to be the first, the most vociferous and the most condemnatory in aggravating unjust and untrue accusations. In the trials of the Salem witches, the Communist baiting of the McCarthy era and the current obsession with sexual harassment, few public leaders have dared to hint that an accused associate might conceivably be innocent. But such cowardice comes at great cost. Unless leaders in the helping professions—medicine, law, teaching, ministry and others—support the many dedicated colleagues who are now being falsely accused by overtly delusional and/or blatantly greedy plaintiffs, all of us will be at risk in an epidemic of vilification popularized by the media.

Chapter 6

Perspectives and Proposals

Christine McGuire Masserman

I have described our experience with IPS-APA at some length because private professional associations have come to function as quasi-legal bodies whose decisions may directly or indirectly cause physicians and others to lose their licenses to practice, lawyers to be disbarred, elected officials to be expelled from their offices and other professionals to be deprived of their basic livelihoods. However, despite their powers, these bodies are rarely accountable for their actions: they are not required to comply with commonly recognized legal standards in obtaining evidence and evaluating its validity, nor do they observe procedural safeguards essential to the protection of persons falsely accused in our greedy, litigious society. The ethics committees of these organizations, may and often do, as in our case, invite complainants and "witnesses" to offer rumor, gossip and/or paranoid delusions as evidence; nor need these bodies act in accord with the most fundamental principle of justice—specifically, that *a person is presumed innocent until proved guilty beyond a reasonable doubt.*

For reasons of supposed public interest (and self-protection), ethics committees more often act on exactly the opposite principle, requiring the victim of false allegations to establish *innocence* beyond doubt, thereby assigning to the accused a task that is almost always both theoretically and practically impossible to accomplish: to "prove" that something *never* happened. Further, the customary method of designating membership on ethics panels typically fails to assure objectivity and impartiality; rather, it practically guarantees that one or more members will be antagonistic to the accused for reasons of perceived rivalry, covert envy, personal aversions, or differences in professional theory and practice. Thus, ethics tribunals may, and often do (as in our case), ignore even the modest procedural regulations (e.g., with regard to the expiration of the maximum interval for making a complaint, establishing the credibility of witnesses, advising the accused fully about the precise complaint against him or her, etc.) of the associations they supposedly represent.

Exacerbating these sources of bias and injustice is the circumstance that, as in so many institutions in a democratic society, members of ethics committees respond to what they feel to be powerful social pressures. The existence of such influences is well illustrated by the assertions that in "The Year of the Woman" (1993), the entire U.S. Senate was "on trial" in its hearings on charges of "sexual harassment" against several senators.

Further, a person improperly censured by a professional association has almost no redress, no matter how egregious the procedural inequities or how unjust the sanctions imposed. In most instances the victim's only recourse is through the courts—a stressful, expensive and usually futile procedure.

The way these nongovernmental organizations function should be of greater concern to *all* professionals, everyone of whom is potentially subject to their jurisdiction. The challenge is to develop institutional arrangements which utilize the expertise of professional associations to protect the public from the relatively few incompetent and/or immoral members, while at the same time protecting the vast majority of highly trained, honorable and dedicated practitioners now at risk from the avalanche of false accusations made by so many seriously disturbed, vicious and/or avaricious patients and clients.

Cloning Accusations

In commenting on the allegations against Jules, much has been made of the fact that, following Ms. Noel's attempts to recruit others and at a time when it was practically certain her case would be settled out of court, two former patients did threaten to join her and were included in the Noel settlement, *at the insistence of the attorney retained by Jules' insurance company.*

This raises two important questions: Why would an insurance company be willing to settle, without any investigation, a couple of potential suits that as far as could reasonably be determined were totally without merit? An obvious answer: To avoid the much greater costs of litigation. A question much more difficult to answer is: Why would two demonstrably grateful former patients, who had been so profuse in their public expressions of appreciation to Jules for their therapy, be willing to join a suit against him? Experienced attorneys familiar with the case respond by pointing out that, at the time, both of these women still owed several thousand dollars for their therapy, and that, as in so many similar situations, a threat to sue for malpractice was a relatively safe and easy way to evade an acknowledged debt. Legal experts add that this is a ploy so frequent that lawyers routinely prepare for an onslaught of suits following extensive newspaper and TV coverage of any allegedly mishandled case. Highly publicized settlements are especially enticing in suggesting essentially pain-free, cost-free, risk-free opportunities for rich malpractice awards.

But reciprocal power and monetary gain are not the sole attractions in sexual harassment cases. Widely publicized allegations of such transgressions invite imitative accusations from suggestible plaintiffs who then recruit others. As a prominent colleague wrote Jules:

> Once the large body of disturbed patients one sees learns that a certain type of complaint has been settled by one's insurance carrier for [large sums] without going to trial, the filing of further complaints by the dishonest, borderline or their hungry plaintiffs' attorneys is virtually assured.

Our correspondent indicated, as have many others, that it was a tribute to my husband's skill and integrity that so few succumbed to temptation, from among the many hundreds of seriously ill patients a person of his prominence would have treated in a lifetime of highly regarded practice.

Why the Pandemic?

People who have never been through such an experience often find it extremely difficult to comprehend how adverse circumstances feed on themselves and thus how totally blameless individuals can become the innocent victims of blatantly false allegations. Unfortunately, it is not unusual. Shortly after the first publicity about the Noel settlement, we received an empathetic letter from a former officer of a district branch of the American Psychiatric Association. It read, in part:

> I have no doubt of your innocence.... Unfortunately, your fate is not rare. I have official and personal knowledge of about 20 colleagues, including other department chairmen or men of similar rank who have suffered a similar fate. In all instances they assumed that their innocence would be sufficient defense, and like the denizens of the gulag archipelago, sought competent legal help too late to be of assistance.

But even our correspondent's numbers give no indication of the extent of the problem. Recent data from attorneys who specialize in this field of litigation indicate that practically all physicians in this country "can count on being named in at least one lawsuit during their lifetime that will DESTROY their financial dreams" (Collander & Gillen, P.C., Naperville, IL); most will be sued multiple times, and the average physician can expect to be sued five times during his or her professional life (Milton & Burningham, Salt Lake City). It is reasonable to expect that a very substantial proportion of these suits will charge ethical misconduct and many of those will allege sexual transgressions.

Nor is the epidemic of false allegations of sexual misconduct limited to physicians and other therapists. In the *Chicago Tribune* of October 30, 1992, Barbara Brotman reports that in order to protect men from false accusations of rape, the National Center for Men has developed a "Consensual Sex Contract" for couples to sign, which outlines each party's specific expectations in a relationship. She quotes Mel Feit, Executive Director of the Center, as saying: "We believe there is an epidemic of false rape accusations. Your reputation can be destroyed for life.... False accusations are devastating for men even if police conclude there is not enough evidence to prosecute."

Experts in the field contend that the same situation is also occurring with regard to child abuse (Chapter 8). Laura Shapiro of *Newsweek* (April 19, 1993) cites a study by the National Committee for Prevention of Child Abuse which "shows that nearly three million children were reported as suspected victims last year [1992]. However, as in the past, fewer than half those reports were found to merit further investigation." She quotes Elizabeth Vorenberg, President of the National Coalition for Child Protection Reform, as saying: "Children get placed in foster care when it is not necessary, cases of real abuse go undetected and people are wrongly reported as abusers. The system fails everybody." According to Sharman Stein of the *Chicago Tribune* (April 7, 1993), the same view is echoed by Martin Guggenheim, a director of the National Coalition for Child Protection Reform, who contends that "there is a lot of over reporting going on." Myriads of child welfare experts reinforce this position and argue that the large number of false allegations of child abuse are seriously handicapping the agencies' efforts to protect children who are really in danger.

The recent upsurge in false allegations of sexual misconduct, especially rape and child abuse, can best be explained on the basis of the existing legal, economic and social systems which, together with our current cultural orientations, conspire to provide large monetary rewards, as well as power and notoriety, to those who persecute others. Consider the following data.

An Increasingly Litigious Society. Legal friends have confirmed my inference from sociological studies that there is more litigation in relation to the size of the population in this country than in any other nation. In a recent column in the *Chicago Tribune,* Kathy Kristof (June 4, 1993) quoted legal authorities as saying that "one lawsuit is filed every thirty seconds in the United States... and roughly one in every ten adults gets sued every year." This flood of litigation is attributable to a number of interrelated factors: our relative affluence, the extraordinarily large number of lawyers competing for clients, the adversarial nature of our legal system in which the goal is to win—not necessarily to discover the truth, and the consequent irrationality of widely publicized jury awards (e.g., $4.3 million to a mugger wounded while trying to escape police following his robbery and attempted murder of a seventy-one-year-old man, $15 million to a factory worker whose termination for alleged theft of a $39 phone was publicly announced on plant bulletin boards, etc.; see also Chapter 8). This system constitutes an urgent invitation to litigation, because anyone can file a suit, charging almost any transgression, against almost anyone, at virtually no cost, risk or inconvenience. Such suits, especially those involving currently fashionable, but nevertheless potentially devastating, allegations of sexual misconduct (which are difficult to defend because the nature of the crime is such that there are rarely any witnesses), are potentially exceedingly profitable to both the accuser and his or her contingency fee attorney.

Sexual Harassment Is the Fad. Fashions change: In seventeenth century Salem (Chapter 7) visions of witches in every shadow were in vogue; in the 1950s, a Communist in every closet was all the rage; currently, allegations of sexual harassment are in style. In some social environments and in some workplaces a woman without her own story of sexual harassment is covertly pitied as unhappily repulsive; in denial, male co-workers, especially supervisors, become likely targets of false accusations.

Equally popular in many circles are "recovered memories" by troubled adults of (fantasied?) childhood abuse by family and friends, and the "release" of repressed "memories" of more recent (imagined?) sexual attacks by advisers, therapists, supervisors, colleagues and ex-lovers. This alleged "bringing to the surface" of so-called "forgotten traumata" has become so widely acceptable as an explanation of personal maladaptations that Dr. Benjamin Lee, a prominent psychiatrist in Salt Lake City, calls it "a growth industry for poorly trained psychologists, social workers and other therapists" (see also Chapter 8). So prevalent has this situation become that innocent victims are banding together to protect each other against gullible therapists who have proved prolific in stimulating these false "memories" in their clients. For example, in 1992 the False Memory Syndrome Foundation was established in Philadelphia to support and counsel family members accused of incest on the basis of "recovered memories" and to "interject some calm into the hysteria"; within one year of its organization the Foundation required thirty volunteers just to field the calls from victims of these accusations (Bonnie Miller Rubin, *Chicago Tribune*, May 30, 1993), some of whom are filing malpractice suits against the therapists allegedly responsible for the "recovered memories" (Anne Wilson, *Salt Lake Tribune*, October 16, 1992). Indeed, false allegations of sexual misconduct have become so nearly ubiquitous that many insurance companies now refuse to indemnify professionals against such charges.

Changing Gender Roles. Historically, rapid change has produced insecurities and uncertainties, and the abandonment of traditional codes of conduct before adequate new ones are fully evolved. Such has been the consequence of the relatively sudden emergence of women in new roles in the workplace, the arts and politics. Some women's organizations argue that this shift, together with the activities of "consciousness-raising groups" over the past twenty years, has led to "a great social revolution." Most observers would agree that a concurrent loosening of generational ties, an increasing dependence on the peer culture to set behavioral standards, and the pervasive changes in sexual mores have resulted in increased libidinal freedoms and confusion among all groups as to what constitutes culturally acceptable behavior between the sexes. Consider the following especially provocative instances: the requests by some men's groups to help them define the line between complimenting a woman and harassing her; the campus code at a major university which defines "rape" as including merely "unacceptable" gestures, glances and/or language; and the posters put up by a group of women at the University of Maryland with the heading: "Notice: These Men Are Potential Rapists," followed by a list of the names of *all* male students at the University (*Chicago Tribune,* May 9, 1993).

Village Gossip and Media Competition. Voyeurism and salacious interest in the affairs of others are not new to our culture: witness the paleolithic Venuses and the cave paintings of Neolithic times. But the technological developments that created the global village have made it immensely profitable for newspapers, magazines, book publishers and radio and TV commentators to cater to the most prurient tastes worldwide. In the competition to command the largest audiences and under the protection of our First Amendment, media moguls rush to spread denigrating current gossip about any prominent person. These pornographic morsels are soon picked up and widely circulated by the mainstream press, usually with an evasive attribution of the slanderous material to the tabloids. The stakes are too high, and the pressure on profits from the competition too great, to be resisted even by serious publications. And so, in a frenzy exceeding that of hungry piranhas, we witness noisy trials by the media that constitute a travesty of journalistic justice.

At a recent luncheon of the Chicago Bar Association held to honor him, Joseph Cardinal Bernadin expressed great concern that the rights and reputations of accused people be respected and protected, and that the presumption of innocence be maintained, lest blameless victims lose their good name, their liberty and their future (Michael Hirsley, *Chicago Tribune,* May 5, 1993). Regrettably, some months later the revered Cardinal was himself victimized.

The Price We Pay

For the victims and their families the cost of false allegations can be horrendous. In addition to the sleepless nights, physical debilitation, social embarrassment and severe emotional toll such charges levy, they have, in many instances, led to bankruptcy, destruction of promising careers, forfeiture of all opportunities to earn a fair livelihood, and even prolonged loss of liberty. As Bert Lance, White House advisor to President Carter, writes movingly in his book, *The Truth of the Matter,* reporters and others continue after some fifteen years to remind people regularly of the allegations of financial mismanagement made against him, but rarely add that he was fully cleared of all charges.

And so it has been for us. As an insightful colleague wrote:

> When Barbara Noel's book is subjected to proper standards and the lurid bright orange color is removed from the cover, and the title suitably modified by a more honest editor…her allegations evaporate.

In short, my husband has never been found guilty of any sexual transgression in any court or legal review, yet this has never been reported by the newspapers, Ms. Watterson, Ann Landers, any talk show, or even the *Psychiatric News.*

Moreover, the rudeness of some reporters has been shocking. For example, when Ms. Watterson first called I explained to her that my husband always declined telephone interviews because of their potential for serious misinterpretation, and I gave her the name and telephone number of the insurance attorney who had arranged the Noel settlement. Ms. Watterson refused to contact Ms. Davy; instead, she continued to send express mail and to call, sometimes several times a day, with professions of "wanting to be fair," until Jules granted her an interview in our home, as described in Chapter 4. Others, in a transparent bow to "objective reporting," also routinely insisted on immediate interviews by phone, at any hour of the day or night, "to present your side of the story," and then failed to use any of the documented materials we conscientiously furnished to everyone who contacted us.

Despite our efforts to deal courteously and objectively with reporters, authors and radio and TV personnel, continuing media vilification produced another distressing fallout. At times the volume of hate mail and obscene and threatening phone calls grew so great that we put a police watch on the phone and arranged for screening of our mail. Anticipating what I was likely to find, it often took a real effort of will to open the newspaper, turn on radio or TV, pick up the mail or answer the phone. Even today, though the harassment seems to have diminished temporarily, when the phone rings or the mail is delivered, I still take a deep breath, brace myself and offer a little prayer. God has not always seen fit to grant my pleas, but He has given us the strength to deal with what is unavoidable and has blessed us in many other ways.

The Hovering Shadow. Along with hypersensitivity and heightened alertness, victimized persons and their families suffer other, in some ways even more insidious, long-term psychological effects. For those deeply hurt by cumulative injustices—and for their families—there may be an enduring post-traumatic syndrome. Like a monstrous cloud it hangs over everything I do: I can be listening to an enchanting Beethoven quartet, watching a stunning ballet, driving down a lovely country lane bright with the colors of autumn, savoring the ocean breeze from the deck of a graceful sailboat when, suddenly for no apparent reason—except, perhaps, some unexpected lurch of the ship—a nonexistent cloud darkens the joy of being—in this case, at the center of a serene and beautiful seascape. I do not know how to rid myself permanently of these threatening fragments of the past, except to remind myself that I am, indeed, figuratively sailing with Jules in a sturdy ship over a sunlit sea (see Chapter 11).

Social Costs. And society as a whole also pays a terrible price for the excesses in which it currently indulges. Our constitutional right to privacy is dangerously impaired, especially for public figures—whether rock musician or Nobel prize win-

ner. Our critically important right to the presumption of innocence has already been abrogated for many and is in jeopardy
for all. So also, our guaranteed right to trial by a jury of our
peers, *unprejudiced by biased publicity,* may no longer be possible. In highly publicized and emotional cases, trial by media
has all but replaced trial by an objective jury. So serious has this
problem become that high-priced consultants on the "science"
of jury selection are now considered an essential part of an
effective defense team, though they are so expensive few defendants can afford their services.

But the difficulty of finding objective persons to serve on a
particular jury is not the only threat to our liberty from media
excesses. The jury system itself—a system which, however
imperfect, has been called the closest approach to justice ever
invented—is now endangered by media violations of the confidentiality of jury deliberations, heretofore sacrosanct—a condition that legal scholars regard as essential to just and
thoughtful decisions.

Our society can ill-afford these threats to our rights.

Reflections on Reform

In ordinary criminal cases the presumption that a crime
has been committed is rarely questioned; the only issue is
"Who did it?" and the burden is on the prosecution to prove
the accused guilty. In contrast, in cases alleging sexual misconduct the issue is not "Who did it?" but rather "Did it happen,
or is it simply a product of someone's fantasies or cupidity?"
and the accused is assigned the literally impossible task of
establishing innocence by proving that something never
occurred. The individual, familial and cultural costs of this
anomaly are far too high; therefore, after extended consultations with various experts in jurisprudence and sociology, I
submit for urgent consideration the following proposals for

economic, legislative, judicial and intraprofessional reforms.

Economic: Eliminate Monetary Gain. First and perhaps most basic, ways must be found to take the profit out of false accusations—i.e., to remove the financial rewards that now go to the accusers, their attorneys and all those who publicize and promote unfounded allegations. Measures to achieve this goal will need to include specific provisions for the imposition of appropriate penalties on persons who deliberately make false charges against others, and to hold fully accountable both the attorneys who represent such persons in litigation without adequate investigation of the validity of their suits, and those who publicize such actions without simultaneously citing relevant contrary evidence. The penalties must be sufficiently severe to restrain rampant character assassination.

Such deterrence must, of course, be accomplished in ways that do not impair an individual's opportunity to obtain appropriate remedies for demonstrable wrongs. Though it will not be easy to reconcile these seemingly conflicting demands, it is critical if we are to control an epidemic in which everyone is now at risk.

Legislative: Provide Means for Redress. Second, better ways must be found to ensure that the victim of false allegations has access to prompt, inexpensive and effective remedies, including both an adequate platform for responding to the charges and appropriate compensation for the damage they have caused. The goals of this reform cannot be achieved with current libel laws which are biased in favor of the persons who make the false accusations and the press which repeats them. Further, existing libel laws levy such an excessive toll in time, money and stress on slandered persons that few can afford to try to obtain justice under current rules. In commenting on a libel case that has now been dragging through the courts for some ten years, William A. Henry III states (*Time*, May 24, 1993): "No matter the official outcome, in most libel suits everyone loses." What is urgently required is that methods which are neither excessively stressful nor outrageously expensive be developed that make it feasible for victims to obtain prompt and widely disseminated retractions of false charges, as well as adequate monetary awards, including punitive damages, in recompense for the injury they have suffered.

But that alone is not sufficient: It is at least as, perhaps even more, important that victims of false accusations have *immediate* access to adequate means for informing the public about the facts of the matter, without enduring the delay, the stress and the cost of filing suit against their accusers. Consider that within a few hours of having been accused of sexual harassment on national television, then Supreme Court nominee Clarence Thomas was able to come to the same venue and reach essentially the same audience with an immediate, dramatic denial in which he called the allegations against him a "high tech lynching." Similarly, then presidential candidate Bill Clinton and his wife were able to reach virtually the entire U.S. population through major TV networks and the mainstream press, with a prompt response to unsubstantiated allegations of sexual misconduct against him, as did then President Bush in reaction to a rumor about his possible infidelity.

That privilege should not be confined to the prominent and the powerful. What is recommended here is that means be found which make it possible for less famous people who have been publicly victimized by false allegations to get the truth out quickly and to get it widely distributed. This may seem impractical; however, it is worth noting that in the political arena we have taken an important step toward rendering debate more balanced by enacting laws requiring broadcasters to provide equal time to all legitimate candidates. An analogous rule, which provides real opportunity for those unjustly accused to respond to an accuser whose allegations have been extensively circulated, would not only help to restore a damaged reputation, it could also significantly reduce the profits to be made from spreading sensational, but unsubstantiated stories and, thus, might give pause to those who now rush to provide a public platform for false allegations.

Judicial: Ensure "Due Process." Rights supposedly guaranteed to everyone by our constitution are, in the case of victims of false allegations, regularly abrogated in three circumstances: First, as discussed above, the attorneys supposedly representing the accused may not be retained by, or accountable to, them; in a high proportion of these cases the defendant's lawyer is far more likely to be employed by an insurance firm, a hospital, school, church or even the government itself (in the case of court appointed defense attorneys). The interests of the entities which hire and pay these legal counselors may or may not coincide with those of the persons in jeopardy. This problem is epitomized in a statement attributed to an attorney knowledgeable about the Noel case, who reputedly told a reporter quite frankly that such suits are *not* about truth and justice— "they're about money," and an agreement to settle certainly should *not* be construed as a judgment about the guilt or innocence of the defendant—it's merely "an ordinary business decision." Where the potential for such serious conflict of interest is so great, it is especially important that ways be found to protect the rights of the accused who, in such cases have no power to select their preferred attorney or to replace one they feel is not representing them adequately.

Equally critical to the innocent victims of false allegations is the integrity of the jury process. To assure that the system functions properly it is necessary that, during their *in camera* discussions, individual jurors feel free to ask what may seem to be irrelevant questions, to explore alternative ways of interpreting the evidence presented, to express and maintain unpopular positions; and to do so without fear that subsequent revelations in the media about their deliberations will subject them to public ridicule and/or, in the case of highly emotional trials, the risk of bodily harm. At the same time, ways must be found to expose and rectify jury decisions that have been tainted by illegal coercion of jurors, by clear violations of court instructions, by outright bias and prejudice deliberately hidden at the time of jury selection, and by failure of jurors to discharge their constitutional responsibilities for reasons of personal convenience, or concerns about health, family and business difficulties and/or fear of the consequences of refusal "to go along with" the majority. Especially troubling have been the numerous recent reports of jurors who, after the conclusion of a trial have publicly retracted a vote of "guilty," explaining that they were under too much pressure at the time to vote their conscience. In order to protect the accused's rights to "due process," ways must be found to guarantee that juries understand what is required of them and that they perform their duties properly, even if that means imposing sanctions on those who fail to fulfill their legal obligations.

In addition to the regular court system, people who practice a profession or own a small business are often, as discussed above, also subject to the jurisdiction of governmental regulatory agencies (e.g., licensing authorities), and to quasi-legal private bodies (e.g., ethics committees of professional associations) that hold hearings in which they act simultaneously as prosecuting attorneys, judge and jury. Anyone who has ever had an audit by the Internal Revenue Service will understand the implications of that way of functioning. As I have shown, these groups are ill-equipped to conduct unbiased proceedings, to separate rumor from fact and to rule impartially on valid evidence. Yet, as we have seen, there is essentially no recourse for persons subject to their jurisdiction who may be wrongfully deprived of their livelihoods, as well as their reputations, by the rulings of such bodies. Ways must be found to assure that these entities adopt and adhere meticulously to procedural rules that protect the innocent, that they observe reasonable evidentiary standards and that their members are held individually and personally accountable for any deviations that violate the requirements of "due process."

Intraprofessional: Strengthen Ethical Codes. As regards problems arising from false allegations, the professional behavior of greatest concern is that of personal injury lawyers and of journalists in both print and broadcast media.

With respect to the legal profession, better ways must be found to assure that attorneys act as conscientious "officers of the court," while still protecting the legitimate interests of their clients. This will entail a reordering of priorities and will require that, contrary to our present system, professional rewards go to those who seek the truth rather than to those who, however ingeniously, seek to evade or distort it. Even modest steps to modify the consequences of the adversarial system will require the cooperation of law schools, legislators, bar associations, judges and others in the judicial structure who now often find themselves to be (sometimes involuntary) conspirators in a system that delays, subverts and, all too often, denies justice.

Similarly, strengthening journalistic codes will also require basic institutional advances so that contrary to present practice, professional rewards will accrue to those who seek the truth rather than, as now, to those who are first with the most sensational headlines. Illustrative of this problem is the incident a few years ago in which a Pulitzer Prize was awarded to a journalist for what was later discovered to be a completely fabricated account of a ten-year-old drug addict's life on the street.

While a "complete fabrication" is clearly outside the code, there are problems which are more subtle than outright prevarication. In commenting on a closely watched libel suit, William A. Henry III states: "Often, a story that provokes a suit is *legally* defensible yet *morally* tainted," and the defendant in that suit has herself been widely quoted as saying about a previous libel suit: "Every journalist who is not too stupid or too full of himself to notice what is going on knows that what he does is morally indefensible" (*Time,* May 24, 1993). Surely, sanctions should be imposed on such behavior by the profession itself.

Long-Range Considerations

True, we cannot legislate probity and decency; rather, we must educate our youth to understand and accept a new set of values. Our children must learn the difference between what is "right" (i.e., mutually beneficial) and what is "wrong" (i.e., counterproductive), and our institutions and customs must be altered accordingly so as to reinforce throughout an individual's lifetime the principle that it is in no one's ultimate interest for us to prey on each other. Only then can we expect a reduction in the personal, group and national conflicts that some of our current institutions and cultures perpetuate, and the escalating social turmoil this violence both reflects and engenders. Fundamental reforms require basic reorientations in our philosophic, educational, social and juristic systems, as elaborated in Part Two of this book.

Chapter 7

Inquiries and Inferences

I, Jules Masserman, deeply appreciated my wife's devotion and support, and I shared her social concerns. Yet both sentiments reinvoked a restless, lifelong search for self-knowledge and interpersonal understanding. Sample issues:

How could I, presumably well trained and experienced in psychology and psychiatry, comprehend the conduct of a patient who, over a period of eighteen years, had repeatedly expressed her gratitude for my insights and guidance in helping her resolve her serious life crises—but who, during an occupational and postmarital crisis, again expressed her intractable ambivalence toward men by extending a wishful fantasy into a sexual assault?

How integrate the behavior of a professional organization that, for over forty years, had bestowed every scientific and administrative honor on me—and then, after an incomplete and biased investigation (Chapter 3), had expanded the patient's demonstrably false allegations into a chimeric horror?

I propose that one answer lies in a frequently observed sequence of erotic attractions, frustrations, inner guilt, reactive hostility and projected victimizations. An historic example at the small community level, referred to by my wife (Chapter 5) is the following:

In the last half of the seventeenth century, Salem, a Puritanically repressed town in the British colony of Massachusetts, became embroiled in economic, political and religious conflicts. As a source of escape and surcease, some of the denizens of Salem, particularly its rebellious youth, became intrigued by the voodoo lore and symbolically libidinal rituals of a West Indian slave called Tituba. This incurred the wrath of the community's fundamentalist Puritan preachers, who issued warnings against evil seduction, directed especially at teenage girls who had reportedly reacted with sexually suggestive behavior after a session with Tituba. To deny responsibility for this, two of the girls began to claim that, after inhaling mystic fumes, they may have been possessed by demons summoned by Tituba. Questioned further, they identified several older women as also "devil-possessed" at Tituba's seances.

Since the first two girls received clerical and public approbation for their "courageous confessions," they were soon joined by others with similar claims of repentant grace.

All of Salem was soon scandalized and, as directed by the clergy, a newly established Christian Court of Inquiry began to employ testimonial modes of proving associations with Satan, reminiscent of Pope Innocent VIII's *Bull Anno 1480* implementing the biblical injunction "Thou shalt not suffer a witch to live." This papal edict commanded the Dominican monks Johann Springer and Heinrich Kraemer to write the *Malleus Maleficarum* (Witches' Hammer), a manual prescribing tortures most likely to elicit lethal confessions. In accord with the Court's verdicts: between May and October, 1692, Tituba and eighteen other poor, retarded, "unchristian" or similarly unpopular women were hanged as witches, and a score more were penalized or exiled. Many others might have suffered had not allegations begun to involve the Governor's popular wife.

However, news of the Salem massacre, although delayed, horrified communities throughout the colonies, some of which called for the militia to halt the "Protestant heresies" in Salem. But it was not until 1696 that the Massachusetts Legislature finally apologized for having condoned this travesty of human intelligence, decency and responsibility.

It is tempting to discern parallels in the Noel case. To give her every benefit of the doubt, Ms. Noel, having been relieved of a severe panic-depressive state, may have felt a surge of affection for her elderly, long-term therapist in the role of father-surrogate and, in a virtual fantasy, identified him with her own father, who she claimed had made what she interpreted as erotic advances during her childhood and adolescence. She herself later described this hallucinatory state to her examiners as one in which she was unable to distinguish between "dream and reality."(Appendix, Reference 4) However, she then rejected the admission as revealing her own guilty incestuous wishes and reverted, as she had during her therapy, to blaming her father as defensively as possible—e.g., witness Ms. Watterson's book, Ms. Noel's pursuit of TV shows, and the search for ever more public approbation.

Such interpretations of similar cases have been offered in the psychoanalytic literature (Freud, Ferenczi, Tausk) but, since Ms. Noel did not return for therapy, they must remain speculative in her instance.

However, far from speculative are the associations of affection and aggression, as reported interminably by our daily press. Teenage "blind dates" turn into traumatic rapes; homosexual jealousies are fatal to unfaithful partners; romantic grooms become wife-beating husbands and are shot by their long-suffering wives.

The Depths of Aggression. Ancient myths indicate basic contra-erotic hostilities in our nature, defensively attributed to mysterious forces beyond our control. Primitive humans conceived both creative and destructive spirits that "possessed" them; later our religions marshaled both categories more poetically under opposing deities: life-giving Osiris versus saturnine Seth, luminous Ahura Mazda vs. dark Ahrimann, Vishnu the Creator vs. Siva the Destroyer; currently, Omnipotent Yahweh or Merciful Allah are still defied by Satan. Significantly, the more anthropocentrically oriented Greeks attributed both good and evil intents to most of their deities, whether denizens of Olympus or Hades.

Such pseudotheistic concepts have also invaded some psychologic postulates. Sigmund Freud, viewing Austrian youths in their sexual prime marching off to rape, kill and die in World War I, thought it necessary to add to his fundamentally libidinal concept of human behavior a contrary "instinct" for destruction and death, and—with his own penchant for personifying abstractions as Hellenic deities—named these conflicting motivations respectively Eros and Thanatos. Directed outward, Thanatos becomes manifest in rage and violence; turned inward, in masochism and suicide. Since Thanatos always supersedes Eros, mankind is doomed to extinction. Parenthetically, the subtle insights of the Greek and Roman pantheons anticipated Freud by two thousand years: Venus Aphrodite, goddess of venery and mother of Eros, was the mistress of Mars, god of war.

Biologically, a "death instinct" seems inferentially valid: most animal species are governed from birth to adulthood by a succession of growth and sexual hormones; however, after full maturity, these are succeeded by catabolic hormones that impair somatic functions and lead to physical debility and death—thus aiding in the survival of the species by preventing overcrowding. So also, adult ants, bees, wolves and members of other species, including human, sacrifice themselves as individuals to sustain and defend their progeny.

And yet, death is not universal and inevitable: Single-celled bacteria and amoebae and organisms of less than eight cells (e.g., rotifers, found in stagnant pools) seem capable of living indefinitely by simple cloning and avoiding growth; indeed, this is figuratively true of unicellular ova repeatedly duplicated as daughter cells in human ovaries. Ergo, to cheer our Freudian friends, we need not perish as a species until the last ovum, through some perversion of Eros, fails to be stimulated to growth by a human sperm.

As the late dean of American psychiatry Karl Menninger once remarked, "our hopes will sustain us"—to the end. Meanwhile man may yet progress, however fitfully, from the designation *Homo habilis,* man the user (and abuser) of tools, toward *Homo sapiens,* man the wise.

PART TWO

Social Turmoil

Chapter 8

Cultural Discords

Part One recounted the personal and familial travails caused by a false sexual accusation, described the disruptive spread of such allegations, and proposed essential reforms in our juristic and social systems. Part Two will present instances of the current urgency of such reforms and for breadth of perspective will then trace the biologic origin, evolution and history of sexuality, its varied esthetic, philosophic, moral and religious implications, and its frequent association with physical violence. Recommendations supplementary to those in Part One will then be made in the interest of future generations.

Present Incentives for Sexual Accusations

For immediate relevance we can correlate the avalanche of sexual accusations with other current problems in our society: pervasive greed, competitiveness, mutual distrusts and litigiousness, with readily available victims. Culled from the daily press, the following examples epitomize the motivations for sexual charges in this cultural climate and the difficulties in meeting them.

Monetary Gain and Notoriety

It is significant that many such allegations are made against prominent and presumably wealthy physicians, entertainers, athletes or others heavily insured (such as priests, supported by the wealth of the Catholic Church). This trend has been intensified by the willingness of insurers to avoid years of expensive litigation by settling even the most outrageous suits out of court for large sums—"settlements" that can be devastating to the falsely accused by being publicized as proving their guilt. Since there are relatively few instances of lawyers being penalized for knowingly filing wrongful charges, more plaintiffs are readily induced by more lawyers, some not averse to paid advertisements designed to engage more clients to bring more suits for ever larger sums. The following excerpts from the current press (with identities ethically eliminated) are illustrative:

> A female psychoanalyst was sued by the family of a medical student who had committed suicide because she had allegedly permitted him to become "overly attached" to her during six years of treatment. The charge could never have been proved, and though there were many different and demonstrable reasons for the suicide, after widely publicized hearings the family nevertheless received an out-of-court insurance award of one million dollars and the analyst sacrificed her medical license.

> A drug company awarded over two million dollars to the family of a convicted murderer, on the grounds that he had presumably been under the influence of a drug manufactured by the company, that is widely prescribed as a sedative.

Frequent reports of such cases are finally eliciting increasingly explicit condemnations by conscientious jurists. Thus, Justice James Heiple of the Illinois Supreme Court in a dissenting opinion about such an award wrote:

"[These verdicts demonstrate] once again the casino-like atmosphere of our tort system....What we are witnessing here is a vast predatory movement of citizen against citizen, the magnitude of which is beyond calculation....Though selected individuals are being made rich, most notably the plaintiff's personal injury lawyers, society as a whole is crippling itself."

About a later instance he added:

"This case is illustrative of the irrational tort system under which we operate....By refusing to recognize any limits on such damage awards, litigants, with the assistance of their attorneys, are turning our court system into a giant gambling casino." (*Chicago Tribune,* January 13, 1993)

However, monetary gain may be absent, or only secondary to other motivations such as the following:

Perversions of Child Abuse (Appendix, Reference 10)

With regard to allegations of the sexual abuse of children and ensuing social victimizations, an especially troubling travesty of human reason and justice was described in successive two-hour broadcasts over the PBS television network on June 21 and 22, 1993. The scene was the previously peaceful and friendly town of Edenton, North Carolina, where a child-care facility, prophetically named "Little Rascals Day Care Center," served an ostensibly neighborly community of about five thousand. However, troubles began when a mother complained to authorities that a staff member at the Center had "slapped" her four-year-old son, and wished the event investigated. The complaint was publicized as an instance of possible sexual abuse, whereupon the mothers of other preschool children enrolled in the Center joined in a clamor for its investigation, even though none of their progeny had described any form of mistreatment.

A self-styled, nonmedical "child therapist" was engaged to examine, "evaluate" and, if necessary "treat" seventeen of the children. By admittedly repetitious and suggestive questions, with instructions to the parents that the inquisition be continued at home, she was apparently able to persuade some of her youngest "clients" that they had indeed been sexually mishandled.

The co-director of the Center and his wife were promptly arrested and, since neither could provide bail exceeding a million dollars, both were imprisoned for over two years awaiting their separate trials. At each hearing, nationally prominent physicians and psychiatrists testified that they had found no indications that any of the children had been physically or psychologically abused, and a succession of lay observers reported under oath that during many unscheduled visits to the Center all the children had been content and many had been enthusiastic about their early training programs. But then the state's three prosecuting attorneys put a series of the "child therapist's" recent or current young "clients" on the witness stand and, with the judge's permission, plied them for extended periods with specifically leading questions such as the following:

> (To a boy) You told Ms.___ [the therapist] that Mr. B___ [the co-director of the Center] kept putting his ding-dong in your mouth. Was that true? [leaving an impression on the jury that the child's induced tale to the therapist and the suggested fellatio were both factual.]
>
> (To a girl) When Ms. D___ [a staff member] put her fingers into your front private parts it hurt, didn't it? [thus avoiding a possible denial that the introitus had occurred.]

To such queries most children replied with a routinely compliant "Yes, sir"; when further questioned as to why, after repeatedly suffering such bizarre and painful experiences, they had not described them to their parents, they again responded with a variable but manifestly prerehearsed explanation to the effect that "Mr. B___ said he would kill Mommy and Dad if I told them."

The parents, on direct examination, said that they understood why their children had remained silent and, in retrospect, now realized that "they must have been deeply disturbed." The prosecution rested its case in Ms. D___'s trial by submitting for the record the therapists' clinical notes, unread in the Court, as presumably supportive evidence, secure in a judicial ruling that since none of the therapists had appeared at the trial, the validity of their examinations and pejorative inferences could not be challenged.

However, gentle cross-examinations of the children by defense attorneys elicited dramatic accounts of events at the Center that had previously not been so well coached. Samples:

> One child voluntarily informed the Court that Mr. B___ liked to stab babies and throw them away and that he had seen many killed.
>
> A second youngster described sexual experiences away from the world in the Center's spaceship.
>
> A third, more nautically minded, recounted his excursions on Mr. B___'s boat, and recalled that when Mr. B___ threw a little girl from his boat into the river to feed some pet sharks, he (then a child hero at age two) had dived overboard and saved her.

The parents were also cross-examined, and when confronted with their own confusions and self-contradictions resorted to a standard reply to the effect that "it was a stressful time two years ago, when my child was being abused, so I can't sort out all the details." Nevertheless, all such indications of the incredibility of the evidence for the prosecution seemed to have little influence. The jury in Mr. B___'s trial, after deliberating for many weeks, returned a verdict of guilty on all but one of approximately one hundred counts of child abuse; when questioned afterward three jurors readily confessed that since the judge had repeatedly requested a unanimous verdict, they had, against their reason and conscience, given in to the others out of sheer exhaustion. So also, the jury in the trial of Ms. D___ , who had courageously refused to plea bargain, found her guilty on all counts. The co-director of "the Little Rascals Center" received the tragically absurd sentence of "twelve consecutive terms of imprisonment for life," and the young Ms. D___the sex-discriminatory kindlier (sic) verdict of a single life sentence, with parole possible after only twenty years. At this writing (1993) the co-director's wife and other staff members are still awaiting trial.

Aftereffects were widespread. The "child therapists" were roundly criticized by highly trained professional colleagues. Intelligent jurors remained troubled about their evasion of human responsibilities, and Center staff members on bail and still awaiting trial are all the more bitter and despondent. Some of the families called to testify became maritally discordant.

But most deplorable of all may be the persistent traumatic effects on some of the "Little Rascals" of their experiences not at the Center, but during their "therapy" and appearances at the trials of Mr. B___ and Ms. D___—trusted caretakers who, they were told, can deceive, misuse and harm them. The only children who were reported to show no adverse effects were those whose parents had refused to subject them to disruptive inquisitions and "therapies."

Recommendations as to rational and effective procedures with regard to accusations of the sexual abuse of children are deferred to Chapter 10.

Personalized Resentments that Occasion Accusations

Protests here range from the borderline absurd through the marginal to the eminently justified.

Preteen dignity. Local, state and federal investigations were launched in response to a demand by a seven-year-old girl who charged "that her right to freedom from harassment had been violated by boys on the school bus who used naughty language" (George Will, *Newsweek,* December 14, 1992).

Numerical sensitivity. Girls in a California high school instituted a suit against male classmates whose publicized claims of dozens of sexual conquests among them ("scores") had been "greatly exaggerated" (sic) (NBC, March 10, 1993).

Pro bono publico. Female naval aviation pilots properly protested harrowing sexual molestations by male colleagues in their Annual Tailhook Convention, and justifiably placed more than a hundred junior and senior naval officers in jeopardy of losing their rank and/or commissions.

Vengeance

Aggression against a person who frustrates a sexual relationship directly or tangentially is also a frequent motivation.

A mistress, rejected after years of a complaisant sexual liaison, claimed that she had been "only a good friend" with her lover until "he raped me again," even though she had forgiven him the first time.

A wife, seeking relief from a loveless, childless marriage and desiring separate maintenance, charged her husband with rape because he "compelled" her to submit to intercourse by denying her various needed privileges and recreations if she refused.

Direct Corrective Action: Juristic

A wife who also felt "raped" by her husband, cut off his penis and threw it into a nearby field. It was found and surgically reattached, with the promise of return of function in a year or two. Both were indicted on sexual assault charges. In separate trials both were judged not guilty—he of rape, she of mayhem.

Other Connations

A female employee, discharged after repeated citings for inefficiency by several supervisors, claimed she was "really fired because I refused to let the boss [have sex with] me the first week I worked at the place." (*Chicago Tribune*, October 9, 1992)

Suits because a written agreement between an engaged couple guaranteeing marriage had been broken by one of the partners. (*Chicago Tribune*, October 16, 1992)

A mother, artificially impregnated with her husband's semen before their divorce, sued her obstetrician for support of her child because he had failed to secure the husband's written consent. (*Chicago Tribune*, January 12, 1993)

Deliberate Falsehoods

Many accusations of sexual misconduct made by women, variously motivated as above, are fabricated and later admitted to be so:

A housewife who had falsely accused an interior decorator of rape later admitted she made the charge up to get attention from her husband. (*Chicago Tribune*, June 15, 1990)

A female member of the Texas Corps of Cadets who had been denied special privileges accused several male cadets of "harassments and attempts at assault" and then retracted her charges—but only after the accused had been suspended or expelled. She herself was not penalized. (*Chicago Tribune*, January 20, 1993)

During a period of eighteen months, over a dozen men were released after up to eight years of imprisonment when women confessed that they had falsely charged them with sexual assaults, or when newly developed DNA or other laboratory techniques proved that the charges had been untrue. (*Newsweek*, January 11, 1993)

Induced Falsehoods

Finally, women placed under mild anxiety-relieving sedation may later accuse their dentists or physicians of sexual transgressions. Relevant research conducted by Dr. John Dundee at Queens University was reported to the American Society of Anesthesiology as follows:

Charges of abuse while under [mild] anesthesia may be the result of drug induced hallucinations.... A review of eighteen cases in which female patients complained of fondling of breasts or "wandering hands" showed that in thirteen cases sexual abuse could not have occurred because a third person was always present, and in two other cases the allegations were physically impossible. (*Chicago Tribune*, November 11, 1990)

Summons to Trial

Despite such miscarriages of justice, there are various wide-spread pressures to bring charges of malfeasance even when questionable or knowingly false. Examples by age:

Adolescent. A fifteen-year-old girl was held in juvenile detention for contempt of court because she *refused* to accuse a teacher of a sexual assault. (*Chicago Tribune*, March 20, 1993)

In a letter to "Dear Abby," a columnist who advises the lovelorn, the writer stated: "I got mad at a friend and accused him of raping me. I didn't mean for it to go as far as it did, but my father got into the act and there was no backing down. My friend is now serving time [in jail].... Is there a solution?" Advice: Confess. (*Chicago Tribune*, June 15, 1990)

Adult. Dorothy Rabinowitz, a keen observer of the sexual scene, reported a clear call to feminine duty from a high academic tower:

There are... certain charges, prime among them sex abuse...that are now considered sufficient unto themselves, and beyond question, simply because they have been brought.... It apparently violate[s]... politically progressive orthodoxy to suggest that a person charged with sex abuse might be innocent. To grasp the mind-set at the heart of this view, we need only recall the words of Catherine Comins, assistant dean of student life at Vassar, who told Time magazine in 1991 that women shouldn't have to concern themselves with being right when they charge someone with rape. Indeed Dean Comins explained, "men unjustly accused might have a lot of pain, but it is not pain I would necessarily have spared them." (*Wall Street Journal*, April 15, 1993)

Regrettably, Dean Comins seems to endorse a memorable maxim I once saw pinned on a Vassar faculty bulletin board:

"You can bring a girl to Vassar, but you can't make her think. [Signed] A Sophomore"

Spin Control

Lessons from an Experienced Flight Instructor

Nevertheless, false sexual accusations especially against health professionals, multiply and cause deep personal sorrows in a climate of social mistrust. In the nine years since the adverse "settlement of the Noel case" and its disastrous ensuing publicity, many sympathetic colleagues have informed me about their experiences with similar professional and social injustices and their attempts to reverse or alleviate their destructive effects. Their experiences and mine have led to the following inferences:

Inference 1—Conflicts of Interest. As noted earlier (Chapters 2 and 6), insurance attorneys operate to the advantage of the insurance firms who retain them, and not necessarily in the best interests of the firms' accused clients who, on investigation, are often shown to be innocent. If a computer printout indicates that, on actuarial grounds, the cost to the firm is likely to be far less than that of the years of litigation required to secure a favorable court verdict, an out-of-court settlement will be made, regardless of its implications of client culpability.

Inference 2—Art in Advertising. The plaintiff's lawyers may assent to a "gentlemen's agreement" to keep the settlement confidential, but unless provision is made for enforceable penalties for violating the agreement, many will then publicize it as widely as possible as their victory—with their names and telephone numbers furnished for the convenience of future plaintiffs.

Inference 3—Truth to Tell. Protests about gross misstatements or stark untruths may produce only minimal results. Example: When *McCall's* Magazine published such material, in a spirit of journalistic research, I wrote an objectively phrased Letter to the Editor, citing evidence (see Chapters 1 and 5) that there had been no "sexual assault" other than in Ms. Noel's fantasies and Ms. Watterson's salacious elaborations. As noted elsewhere this letter received only delayed and condensed publication.

Inference 4—Visual Enhancement. Many colleagues have reported that their appearances on TV programs have proved counterproductive.

Over the preceding years I had, with moderate frequency, participated in TV discussions confined to professional topics, but after the publication of Ms. Watterson's book, results with regard to the Noel nightmare were dubious. Ms. Noel had presented her story on talk shows throughout the country, and I had received many invitations to reply. I accepted only two—one from CNBC and the other from CNN—both on condition that I be interviewed only by telephone. In each case the results were greatly disconcerting: Ms. Noel, televised in person, was given nearly fifteen minutes to present her lurid account, and I was accorded two or three for replies mysteriously interrupted and then abruptly terminated, ostensibly by "technical difficulties." Heartened by indignant letters from viewers of both programs, a month later I accepted a third invitation from CNBC, and, as described in Chapter 4, Christine and I were courteously interviewed in our home, again with due credit to CNBC.

Inference 5—Retribution. Finally, during periods of special stress, I would consider a justifiable recourse to a libel suit against some particularly vicious detractor—but would be deterred by wise and friendly counsel, on the following grounds:

First, concurrent costs. Television networks and publishers of newspapers, magazines and books retain corps of attorneys who can compound evidence, postpone trials for years, and then appeal adverse verdicts interminably while enjoying the spectacle of the original plaintiff in bankruptcy.

Second, current juristic concepts and procedures. Verdicts by modern judges and juries as to guilt or innocence are no longer dependent, as they were in the Middle Ages, on whether the alleged malefactor when heavily weighted in chains and tossed into the nearest river, sank in divine grace or, with Satan's help floated and was thereby guilty and deserved being burned at the stake. Instead, a more extensive array of "evidence" is now weighed by social or legal "juries of peers" who decide the earthly fate of the accused. But the term "evidence" raises the vital question as to what is evident to whom?

In our reactively guilty culture, sexual accusations against physicians, ministers, teachers, artists, entertainers, political leaders and other prominent individuals are presumed to be based on "facts," whereas denials are regarded as merely routine; prosecuting attorneys can marshal witnesses at state cost (e.g., over $3 million to convict a young nursery school teacher in New Jersey—Dorothy Rabinowitz, *Wall Street Journal,* April 15, 1993), while the accused must pay for his or her defense, to meet the impossible criterion of establishing *innocence* "beyond a reasonable doubt." To those who wish to doubt and condemn, President Clinton, himself, can never *dis*prove that he had been unfaithful to his wife, Hillary.

Third, current requirements of a libel suit. In our country of free speech, any person can safely malign any other, provided the latter is "sufficiently prominent." Since I have escaped that category, I could legally sue my villifiers, but would still have to conform to other provisions:

Prove I had *not* sexually assaulted Ms. Noel, presumably by a continuous motion picture of my movements since I first met her.

Prove that such charges were made by persons who knew they were untrue and used them for gain or with malicious intent.

Prove that the sums sued for were reasonably commensurate with the losses and suffering caused by the charges, the breadth of their distribution, and their future effects.

Logically, none of these "proofs" could reasonably be established and, if my libel suit ever reached trial, I could not be certain that a sufficiently conscientious judge and jury would render a verdict favorable to me.

Ergo: Do not casually add the burden of libel litigation to the travail of false allegations.

Conclusion: In the interest of self-respect and the integrity of my profession I, with supplementation by Christine, have written this book in the hope that many will join in promoting cultural, juristic and social reforms. One encouraging sign is the letter from the Chicago Medical Society, reproduced on page *xv*.

The next three chapters trace the roots of sexuality, its evolution, its perverse association with violence and its optimal roles in human welfare.

Chapter 9

Sexuality and Violence: Eros and Thanatos

We may now examine more generally and significantly the genesis and biologic evolution of sexuality, its role in the development of human concepts and cultures, the social modes of its control, and the seemingly anomalous association of sexuality with individual and group violence. We can utilize two primary modes of thought: the Kantian categorical and the Comtean developmental.

Categorical. Immanuel Kant (1724-1804), with a characteristic Teutonic bent to sweeping philosophic generalizations, distinguished real "things in-themselves" (phenomena) from immaterial ideas or "faiths" that regulate human behavior.

Developmental. Auguste Comte (1798-1857) regarded faiths as attempts to deny ignorance and insecurity, and placed them within the following progress of thought and behavior:

Mystical: Initially, all objects, including human beings, were regarded as imbued with and controlled by unseen forces variously personified as spirits, ghosts, or minor godlets, sometimes subsidiary to an Emperor-God; fortunately, all could be influenced by magic formulae or bribes to serve the faithful.

Classificatory: Attempts were next made to encompass

nature by postulating that all matter is composed of a few basic substances, varying from the classical Greek "elements"—earth, air, fire, and water—to current theories of interacting wave particles. Much more misleading are endeavors to classify human beings.

Dynamic: In this final (?) phase man discerns more clearly complex interrelationships among multiple "causes" and "effects" in all occurrences, with due allowances for Heisenberg's Principle of Uncertainty (i.e., unpredictability), affecting all observation and inference, whether mystical, classificatory or—to complete the cycle—"scientific."

Fundamental uncertainties in all three modes, as to the creation and purpose of the universe and of mankind, have given rise to contentious formulations ranging from unfaltering faiths in unquestioned religious revelations to graded reliance on continuously researched "scientific evidence." Yet these seemingly incompatible seekings for certainty, as do all others in between, inevitably combine Kantian faiths with Comtean modes of thought. Witness the following comparative analysis:

Theism

It is well to be alert to the precarious nature of any discussion of what Comte termed man's earliest way of disclaiming responsibility for his behavior; namely, by surrendering its control to supernatural beings, especially when their priests are organized into awesome pantheons served by religious cults that assure every believer a blissful immortality and every dissident an eternity in perdition. In an address to the American Psychiatric Association on "Science, Psychiatry and Religion," I spoke in part as follows:

> Despite the current vogue of freedom in "approaching religion from an analytic point of view," it is still true that an objective discussion of any man's beliefs is tantamount in daring to a similarly searching appraisal of his beloved wife or

his wishfully conceived children. As humanists, we are deeply sensitive to the fact that when any man asks us to evaluate either his faith or his family, he is posing a loaded question, burdened with many weighty codicils. In the case of the less dangerous topic—say, his wife—he has spent a lifetime seeking an ideal companion who can offer ecstatic satisfactions in his youth, esthetic pride in his maturity, comfortable services in his middle years, serenity in his old age, and perhaps even an eternity of posthumous comradeship in a geographically and climatically perfect locale where the marriage had been arranged by a benign Deity in the first place. We recognize that these fantasies about his wife are ever precious, much as they are about his cherished religion. Therefore, a reassurance-seeking query in either field carries with it the implicit plea: "Listen, friend! Some shadow of uncertainty, loneliness, and yearning may have crept into our discussion. But do not dare crudely to impugn either of my faiths, for then I must treat you as a desecrator." (*Progress in Psychotherapy,* Vol. 5, 1959)

Relevance to Sexuality. Every major theologic system includes some account of the origin of human beings and of their search for understanding, amity and virtual immortality through procreation. Consider Moses' revelations direct from his god Yahweh, as recorded in the beginning of the Old Testament, and still regarded by over a billion Jews, Christians and Muslims as Holy Writ.

Sexuality, Biblical

In five days (about four thousand years ago, by medieval ecclesiastical reckoning) omnipotent Yahweh created day and night, the sky and the stars, the earth and all the fish, fowl, and other animals. On the sixth day He breathed life into a male image of Himself—named Adam, and sometime later gave him a female companion named Eve. God promised both permanent existence in the Garden of Eden, provided that they remained blissfully ignorant of what He alone should know and understand. But He also did what has ever since occasioned theologic polemics: He provided Eve with a many branched source of knowledge and a reptilian seducer; then, when Eve acted in accord with God's prescient plan, He expelled both Eve and innocent Adam from Eden, with only two leaves "to hide their [newly discovered] nakedness." As portrayed in Michaelangelo's famous painting in the Vatican, Eve left with a sly half-smile of triumph since she had also acquired a knowledge of sexuality, though not yet of its accompanying fatalism. This was soon manifest in her progeny as a dark legacy to all mankind: endless toil, fraternal envy and treachery, the mark of Cain in the ever present specter of death and, most subtly punitive of all, nagging doubt as to God's benevolence. Thus, very early, sexuality became associated with uncertainty, anxiety, vicious aggression and mortality.

No bibliophile can fail to be charmed by the elegance of the King James text from which the above account is derived; nor can a perceptive one be less than intrigued by its allegorical profundity. With regard to evolutionary logic (see below) light, sky, earth, the waters and the lesser forms of life would be created before God would lend His image to man. The ensuing poesy then epitomizes the blessedness of life if conducted in accord with divine edicts, and the folly of prying too deeply into transcendent mysteries, including those of mortality and creativity. Thus the wisdom and warning of the Pentateuch.

Sexuality, Evolutionary

In a less obvious form of faith—confidence in the reliability of human observations, the infallibility of logic and the validity of inductive inferences—man has postulated varied fanciful versions of the genesis of life as being merely incidental to physical conditions favorable to the synthesis of progressively more complex organic compounds—a process that could be occurring throughout the universe. The current account runs about as follows.

Ten (or twenty?) billion earth-years ago, a primordial Source of Infinite Energy (God?), in an infinitesimal fraction of pre-time, released unimaginable quadrillions of stars to initiate and illuminate curved space-time with nuclear brilliance, each sun being destined to fade into an unfathomable "black hole" before being resurrected as part of an eternal Cycle of Creation. Five (or ten?) billion years after what cosmologists affectionately call the "Big Bang," much of the stardust gravitated into luminous spiral constellations, one of which we now call "our" Milky Way. On one of its outer arms there appeared an incandescent sphere we call "our" sun, and out of the gaseous clouds surrounding it, nine (?) orbiting planets emerged, the third nearest the sun being "our" Earth.

As it, too, cooled, its wave-particles coalesced, first into atoms of hydrogen (one electron circling one proton), then helium (two of each), and progressively into a multiplicity of increasingly complex compounds. Those containing carbon were capable of absorbing ("feeding on") other stable atomic assemblies (molecules) to form increasingly large, complex and environmentally reactive "organisms" in the form of primal bacteria or mobile amoebae. These in turn could exchange molecules (have "proto-sexual intercourse") with other similar but not identical organisms, and then clone to generate new ones slightly different from each of the "parents." The intermediate progenitors of life were chemical compounds called amino acids, which combined to form RNA (ribonucleic acid) a messenger for cell structure—a process later elaborated by DNA (chains of deoxyribonucleic acid) that assembled, differentiated and integrated cells into progressively more complex organisms. Sections of these chains (chromosomes) contained the specialized sex genes (female XX or male XY in humans) which then evolved and dominated both the plant and animal kingdoms, and regulated behavior, including reproduction, from birth to senility. Since only the most sturdy and adaptable of the progeny could survive to generate ever new varieties of life, three billion years of selective evolution produced the wondrous range of creatures that now share "our" Earth.

Significantly, the sexuality that emerged in the planet's primal oceans is still manifest in the lunar-tidal cycles of preparation for coitus and procreation in higher organisms. About every twenty-eight days a neural center (the hypothalamus) in every woman's brain commands a nearby master gland (the pituitary) to send into the blood stream a hormone that causes one of her ovaries to release a female sex cell (ovum, containing an XX gene) into a conduit (the Fallopian tube) to her uterus. On its way, the ovum can select and unite with one among millions of male cells (sperm, with an XY gene) that had been deposited during sexual intercourse. The fertilized egg (gamete) then embeds itself in the womb to initiate the miraculous development of either a female (with a genetic XX chromosome) or a male (with an acquired XY chromosome) human being.

Sexual Aggression. For semantic clarity, the term "aggression" does not necessarily connote violence; as derived from Latin *a-greso* it implies only "to go toward." Thus, when an ovum moves to incorporate a sperm which swam to meet it, neither is violated; on the contrary, they can live indefinitely in their progeny and so serve the survival of the species.

Sexuality, Violent. Sexual aggression in this sense, however, implies the injury or destruction of one partner by the other, and soon appeared in the evolutionary process. In *The Biologic Roots of Human Behavior,* I cite instances such as the practice of female praying mantis and black widow spiders feasting on the males during and after impregnation. (Biologists rarely resist commenting: "Consumed with love at the nuptial feast.") Among mammals, male mink bite and may seriously wound females during coitus; lower primates may kill and eat small females after mounting; among humans, sadistic foreplay and intercourse are common in both genders. As a gastronomic regression, Marco Polo describes a banquet at which his host, a Mogul lord, offered him a harem beauty—presumably slain for unfaithfulness, baked whole and served on a long silver platter.

Except in the case of egg-laying insects and starving humans (some primitive tribes eat captives), it is difficult to attribute cross-gender cannibalism to special dietary needs. Rapes may be incident to sexual frustrations and homicides committed for concealment, but in other instances sexual violence, sublethal or lethal, is an admixture of erotism with other motivations and reactions discussed in that context later in this chapter. Here relevant to the theme of procreation are the following topics.

Evolutionary Roots of Procreation

Courtship: Among competing males, rituals can become esthetically elaborate, instead of violent. Illustrative of the fantastic decor to attract a mate, the bower birds of Australia and New Guinea build landscaped entries to their future nests, erect maypoles out of sticks, pebbles and seashells, paint them with berry juice or charcoal mixed with saliva, and decorate them with fresh flowers daily. In many species, including man, mating is further facilitated by bodily displays and decorations, species-specific body odors (pheromones), distance-calling clicks or songs, and precoital poses and dances.

Environmental Preparation: No human engineer confined to the raw materials available to a spider, bee or beaver can improve the plan or construction of a spider web, a cocoon, a beehive or a beaver dam, as designed also for the protection and sustenance of mates or progeny.

Parental Care: Self-sacrifice evolved at all levels. Spiders will poison themselves so that their disintegrating bodies can feed their brood of hatchlings; a fleeing gazelle will turn to face a pursuing leopard so that her calf can escape with the rest of the herd; an ailing human mother will seek an almost certainly fatal cesarean operation to save the life of her unborn child. As to paternal participation, a threat to the young of most mammalian species will provoke violent defensive action from both parents.

Frustrations of Procreation

It is a self-evident evolutionary tenet that higher organisms will attempt to evade or remove obstacles to the satisfaction of a basic need. Reactions to sexual restraints may be especially violent. Veterinarians, trainers of large animals, circus performers and zookeepers know that if a male becomes visually or olfactorially responsive to a receptive female of its species, it may become destructive of all restraints and dangerously hostile to its keepers. Usually docile Asian work elephants have to be chained to solidly rooted trees and very cautiously approached during the female rutting (oestral) months; many mahouts who neglected this precaution and relied on previous trusts have been killed. My own research on comparative animal patterns, as reported in my book *Biodynamic Roots of Human Behavior,* extended these field observations to controlled laboratory studies of species ranging from gerbils to primates.

Frustrated Seduction. Oestral animal females may evade coitus with undesirable males, but are not usually attacked if other females are available. However, in many human cultures, especially in Western societies, women compete in dressing and acting invitingly, accept *tête à têtes* in intimate surroundings, drink excessively, and in other ways imply their sexual interests. Yet when men with aroused libidos respond even mildly, they may be charged with "harassment"; flirtatious gestures become "sexual assaults." True, resisted bodily contacts are legal misdemeanors or felonies, and attempts at coitus, whether successful or not, should be severely punishable. Nevertheless, some jurists hold that if the woman had been deliberately and excessively seductive, she is an accessory to the offense, with the man's punishment and her claims for monetary compensation accordingly modified. The latter consideration is particularly relevant if the woman had ardently courted the man as a permanent sexual or marital partner and he had rejected both roles, whereupon she had dramatized the aphorism: "Hell hath no fury like a woman scorned." In this respect, Freud warned his disciple Ferenczi that analogous reactions may complicate prolonged psychoanalytic therapies that "bare the Unconscious," during which a patient becomes libidinally attached to his or her analyst, and regards asexual treatment as personal rejection.

Sexuality in Context

Sexuality may now be considered more broadly as imbuing basic human motivations for vitality, social security and a sense of mystic fulfillment, but superseding none of them. I have expanded this thesis in many previous writings (see Bibliography), here greatly condensed under its anthropologic, historical, social and existential parameters as follows.

Anthropological. One (or more) million years ago, our ancestors evolved from their primate predecessors by developing three distinctively human aptitudes:

The use of fire and tools,

The expansion of modes of communication, and

A wondrous capacity for creative imagery.

As elaborated in the following chapter, these advances were actuated by three ultimate and urgent (Ur) motivations:

Ur I-Physical: For the vitality and skills required to master man's environment;

Ur II-Social: For the sexual and cultural alliances necessary for group hegemony; and

Ur III-Metapsychologic: For the beliefs and faiths essential to serenity.

Historical. In the ensuing millennia mankind sought, and under favorable circumstances attained, various fulfillments of these triune Ur-aspirations:

Physical: From fire and chipped flints we progressed to the development of vast and complex technologies to promote our somatic well-being, comfort and longevity.

Social: Through cohesive communications we organized families and clans into ever larger and internally more cooperative nations and assemblies of nations.

Existential: With poetic visions we fashioned artifacts of inspiring beauty, composed ethereal music, explored far horizons of sciences and philosophies, and formulated esoteric theologies.

N.B. Sexuality, idealized as love (i.e., empathy, devotion, service), contributed constructively to all these Ur-phenomena.

Conversely, under real or fancied deprivations or frustrations, our Ur-strivings have produced perverse effects:

Anti-physical: Our industries have denuded and polluted our planet, induced new diseases and produced weapons capable of obliterating our race.

Anti-social: Spurred by ignorance, greed and paranoid leaders, ever larger communities, from primitive tribes to alliances of nations, have engaged in ever greater mutual devastations.

Anti-existential: The most prolonged and destructive conflicts have been actuated by equally cherished and equally irrational political, cultural or religious convictions on the part of massed belligerents engaged in reciprocal slaughters.

N.B. Sexuality, debased by preemptive greeds, pervading irresponsibilities and displaced adherences to false idols, has degraded individuals, perverted cultures and demoralized nations.

Sexual Frustrations

In this less than instantly accommodating world, all human aspirations—physical, social, spiritual—are destined to meet with some degree of frustration. Behavioral effects will then vary with many factors: the intensity of the need, the possibility of overcoming the intervening obstacle, the resilience of the reactor, the availability of substitutive satisfactions, and many other contingencies, previously discussed. Sexual disappointments, which to those who experience them often seem to involve not only Eros but all three Ur-seekings, may produce particularly severe and unique reactions, the following being of immediate concern.

Suicide. The subtly accusatory reason given for this internalized urge to destruction after an especially traumatic sexual rejection may be contained in a written farewell note to the effect: "I could not live without you." This pathetic dirge apparently expresses an unrequited but profound devotion; but it also has the vengeful counterpoint: "You will now regret your loss and be sorry you caused my death," and even "You may sense my spirit witnessing your sorrows." This latter fantasy springs from a notion of immortality derived from an attendant wishful extrapolation:

> We have all slept, but ever awakened; and we may have been in coma or anesthetized, but always recovered; since there can be no concept outside of experience, death, too, can be conceived only with an eventual return to some form of consciousness and activity. Depending on what we were taught, this may be in various Heavens or Elysian fields as rewards for approved earthly conduct, or on some dreaded purgatory for misbehavior; however, as believed by primitives and prelates alike, we persist in some form, usually as disembodied spirits, perhaps with powers to settle accounts back on Earth.

An NBC newscast on January 27, 1993, presented a poignant association of marital empathy, anomalous violence, death of a beloved wife, her grieving husband's attempt at suicide, his social rescue and care, and an incredible juristic denouement. The drama is here condensed as follows:

> A gentle, well-liked aged couple planned simultaneous deaths because the wife was dying in excruciating pain from a spreading cancer, and the husband, after nearly fifty years of "perfect marriage" really did not wish to live without her. He killed her by hammer blows and asphyxiation, but his own attempt at suicide resulted only in a drug coma. He was revived by friendly neighbors, given excellent medical care—and then confined to a guarded hospital ward not for the treatment of his severe melancholia, but as imprisonment on a charge of premeditated murder.

Homicide. The diverted hostilities of a jealous mistress who shoots her lover's wife, or the wounded honor of a cuckolded husband who kills not his wife but his interloper, are rages more deeply directed, respectively, to the lover and the wife for having precipitated an emotionally unendurable dilemma—one often leading to further homicides or suicides among the survivors.

Genocide. This terror could not be more incisively epitomized with regard to mass sexual aggression than by this quotation.

> Rape and killing are chief among...man's recreations...[and are usually reserved for the nobility]....In war the privileges are distributed to the lowliest foot soldier: every man a king. (Lance Morrow, "Conquest By Rape," *World at Large*, March 1, 1993)

The excerpt is from an article on a then current Balkan conflict in which Serbian, Bosnian and Croatian armies methodically raped tens of thousands of women in opposing territories—a savagery rationalized on the basis of "ethnic cleansing." This perversion of unbounded lust was specifically forbidden in early Mosaic law, but has nevertheless been practiced by militant hordes from Ashurbanipal ("the Assyrians came down like a wolf on the fold") to Hitler's Super-Aryans, and its elimination still awaits the abolition of all wars.

The infinitely more salutary modes of utilizing sexuality for human welfare are explored in the next chapter.

Chapter 10

Reflections and Recommendations

The question then remains: How can we best restore sexuality's optimal contributions to human contentment, continuity and creativity?

There have been many attempts to clarify and resolve the problems involved (Chapters 7 and 9). Freud, for example, implied a basic distinction between creative and regressive drives, by classifying human motivations as either erotic (sexual, parental, socially hegemonous) or thanatic (masochistic, destructive, homicidal). Historically, human societies have differed greatly as to which of these inferred "instincts" are to be freely expressed or strictly controlled: in Emperor Asoka's India (300 B.C.) and in Mandarin China, people reportedly lived peacefully, tranquilly and productively, as contrasted with prescribed barbarism, rape and genocide under an Attila or a Hitler. Some apologists have proposed a clue to such differences: fertile China and lush India provided for vital needs, whereas Attila's starving hordes were promised the plenties of Europe and the luxuries of Rome, and Hitler's *sturmtruppen*, recruited in a supposedly repressed post-war Germany, were to rule an Aryan dominated world where, incidentally, women of inferior races were to be either eliminated or sterilized for restocking "convenience camps."

Nevertheless, since relatively successful societies do emerge (other examples: early Nilotic Egyptian and island Indonesian) and others fail, we may seek to understand the functions of sexuality with reference to the balance of satisfactions versus frustrations of the universal (Ur) aspirations of mankind for survival, security and transcendent serenity in each society.

Dynamic Perspectives

Various social, philosophic and theistic orientations and organizations may now be considered with special regard to sexuality. An historical survey follows.

Social

Early civilizations in Egypt, Mesopotamia, the Indus Valley and China developed into hierarchies ranging from serfs or slaves with virtually no rights, through farmers, merchants, soldiers, bureaucrats and priests with increasing duties and privileges, to an absolute monarch often with divine attributes. Women were held subservient in all echelons except in dynastic Egypt, where an occasional Hatshepsut or Cleopatra could achieve Pharaonic status. Because of the strict social codes prescribed by a Babylonian emperor such as Hammurabi or a delegated vizier such as Kung-fu-tze (Confucius), everyone knew his and her assigned place, obligations and rights, and there were few internal rebellions; significantly, external wars occurred when the desert-living Hittites or Assyrians had to conquer more arable lands to sustain their economies. So also relative peace was maintained in Attica until Athens decided on a futile expansion of trade, and Alexander left poor, mountainous and backward Macedonia to conquer the world—and acquire numerous "princess wives" along the way.

Rigidly stratified social orders, although inherently vulnerable to turmoil in the long run, were transmitted through Rome to Western Europe. The Pope became nearly all-powerful over life on earth and thereafter, as did to lesser degrees his assembly of princes of the Church and subserviently ranked priests; contesting voices, like those of the great Dominican humanist Bruno, were silenced at the stake as late as 1600. On the secular side, monarchs no longer claimed personal divinity, but retained its equivalent in the form of "divine" (i.e., absolute) privileges. Slavery, though ostensibly abolished by Church edicts, was replaced by a system of serfdom in which members of the lowest classes were similarly indentured for life to serve the dictates, whims, and pleasures of variously ranked feudal "nobles"—princeling "cousins" of the king who gave them almost absolute power over their fiefdoms, including sexual misuse of its women and children.

True, there were some reforms in the areas of Scandinavia, the Netherlands, Switzerland and elsewhere, but the English Magna Carta, signed in 1215, still preserved the rights of the nobility and modified only some of the tyranny of King John. Nevertheless, because the feudal system fed and housed, however miserably, the "lower" classes and rewarded the "upper" ones, while still limiting the expectations in all ranks, it remained relatively stable almost until the American and French revolutions proclaimed the "inalienable rights" of all *men* to "liberty, equality and fraternity"—rights not yet specifically accorded to women. (American women did not have the right to vote until 1920.)

Philosophy

Sappho, a sixth century B.C. intellectual, was famed equally for her exquisite poetry and her empathetic resolutions of hostilities among Aegean men and women on the basis of mutual needs. Plato, a homosexual—as were other disciples of Socrates—paid little heed to the role of women in his plan for an hierarchic Republic, ideally—and predictably—dominated by philosophers; he was soon banished from Syracuse, the only city where his system was tried, by King Dionysis who had no intention of being superseded by a self-styled statesman with so little need for women and so naive an understanding of male competitiveness. Augustine, after his youthful Manichean liberalism, substituted the worship of Mary, Mother of Jesus, for his previous reverence of his own mother, Mona, but then seemed to regard all other women as emissaries of Satan, and thus set a Church policy that excepted only a few female saints.

So, also, later philosophers such as Aquinas, Maimonides, Spinoza and Kant likewise colored their tangential references to sexuality with current Christian, Arabic, Hebraic or Teutonic precepts, whereas Karl Marx's solution to problems of gender (and violence) was the abolition of contention over property and, until such time as Communism could be fully established, a system of equal pay for equally valued services—without, however, defining what would be commensurate compensation for what contributions so evaluated. Philosophers, except for a single Ionian female savant, have been remiss in clarifying, let alone resolving, the many individual and social problems of sexuality encountered in various cultures throughout the ages.

Religion

Theology, quite aside from its influence on our philosophies, is the final modality by which we hope to learn the origin and nature of the universe, and the truth about man's genesis and obligations on Earth and in a presumed thereafter. Revelations and instructions from an omniscient and omnipotent god, or gods, as mediated by their priests, are therefore avidly welcomed and followed—an arrangement that has undoubtedly given comfort, security and serenity to billions of faithful mortals, but that has also caused deep anxieties in others who fear the consequences of transgression implied in Jesus' warning: "I bring you not peace, but the sword!"

With regard to sexuality, many religions prescribe a strict code of conduct—one often violated by religious leaders with adverse effects on social morale. As biblical examples, King David's disregard of Mosaic precepts in sending his neighbor Uriah off to war and then seducing his wife, and King Solomon's tyranny and open promiscuity (recorded in his Song of Songs) weakened Israel's theistic solidarity, and hastened its conquest and the first Diaspora.

Religious faiths can also be perverted to meet male desires. In Greece and later in the Roman Empire, virgins were recruited by priests to serve as temple prostitutes, with attendant distress to families and communities not sufficiently devoted to the Greco-Roman pantheon. In medieval Europe some monasteries turned to homosexuality and convents occasionally became notorious brothels patronized by bishops and cardinals. In the Muslim world sultans and caliphs added, to the four wives permitted by the Koran, extensive harems which they periodically freshened by selling (or drowning) unwanted inmates and replacing them with attractive maidens. And through the centuries variously designated priests, monks and nuns have violated pledges of celibacy—a practice of special current concern to the Catholic Church. Religious prohibitions and inhibitions have not invariably resolved the problems of human libido.

Sanctioned Promiscuity

Why not, then, avert such transgressions by permitting "free" sexual intercourse between consenting adults? As late as the nineteenth century in America, Sioux Indians offered sexual access to their wives during a joint winter encampment with members of the Lewis and Clark Expedition to the western territories, and felt honored when the offers were accepted. Such permissiveness has been tried repeatedly in quasi-utopian communities explicitly emancipated from sexual restraints; and all eventually failed because of internal dissension. For example, the disciples of Joseph Smith, calling themselves Latter Day Saints, practiced polygamy, covert concubinage, and provided "wives of the night" for Brigham Young and other traveling Elders of the Mormon Church, a privilege reminiscent of the *droit de seigneur*—the custom that gave feudal lords the right of sexual access to every bride in their domains. Even after this open prostitution was forbidden in 1890 by the Mormon Church, communities that continued to condone former freedoms soon foundered on disruptive jealousies, intense desires for the exclusive possession of sexual partners, doubts as to the paternity of children and conflicts over the care, loyalties and other requirements of enduring familial and social securities. To enter the Union, Mormon Utah accepted constitutional monogamy.

Thus the eventual success of a group of devout, intelligent and resourceful pioneers who founded and amended a missionary faith. Not so the fate of fanatic cults such as the Branch Davidians, led by a libidinally unrestrained rock musician who proclaimed "I will rule the world with the rod between my legs"—and who, while this book was being written, perished in a reportedly self-ignited fire along with about eighty of his disciples, including seventeen children.

Integrations and Applications

The above social, philosophic and theologic analyses imply the following theses: (a) that mankind is actuated not by Freudian sexuality alone, but more broadly by fundamental needs for physical, social and existential satisfactions; (b) that excessive aspirations in all three spheres are doomed to disappointments and frustrations to which human beings may react counterproductively; and (c) that the latter eventuality can be avoided by diminishing expectations to reasonable limits of attainment. The application of these premises to sociocultural progress may now be considered.

Social Reorientations

The first requirement is a sometimes wrenching reappraisal of the facile but misleading adages which purportedly imbue Western "liberal" societies. For example, the injunction "Do unto others as you wish others to do unto you" would justify sexual advances on the premise that the recipient should respond in kind—an arrogant presumption. Disillusioning on a far broader scale is the recognition that the famed banner of the French Revolution—"Liberty, Equality and Fraternity"— proclaims three unrealistic social goals: a society must be based on limiting the economic, sexual and other preemptive "liberties" of its members, no one of whom will be precisely "equal" in strength, intelligence or special talents to any of the others with whom he or she may or may not choose to fraternize.

Much closer to validity is the slogan "To each according to need and from each according to ability to contribute to the welfare of all"—provided that individual "need" and "welfare of all" are contingently defined. To restore a balance between abstract idealism and operational reality, it would be well to concede that every member of any society is basically concerned with his or her own welfare (see Machiavelli and Marx), but that his or her services to others would, nevertheless, be enhanced if he or she also understood that such contributions would be personally profitable—a recognition that, despite cynical disclaimers, makes cooperative human associations possible.

Inequities. Although human societies should be purged of castes (an Untouchable could marry a Brahman, an African-American woman could be elected President of the United

States), every individual should coordinate his or her ambitions with a "realistic" (the quotes admit inevitable subjectivity) assessment of his or her capacities and an "objective" survey of his or her career opportunities and concomitant economic, sexual, marital and procreative satisfactions.

Communications

How, then, reeducate populations traditionally prepared to live among interpersonal and group contentions and hostilities? An obvious objective is to eliminate conflicts insofar as possible, and a clue to this solution lies in the philologic significance of the verb "educate." Derived from the Latin *e-duco*, the term literally means "to lead out"—in this case, the skills we acquired during eons of higher primate communications from which a primeval language evolved. As human groups spread, this language was enriched with different vocabularies, modifiers and idioms, but since it continued to reflect the perceptive-cognitive-action functions of our brains, which remained identical in all "races," cultures and civilizations, all derived languages, including the thousands now in use are, as famed linguist Noam Chomsky demonstrates, mutually translatable, understandable and potentially persuasive. Further, since all human beings seek essentially similar physical, social and psychologic securities, they would be correspondingly receptive to sincerely and appropriately phrased explanations about limiting their aspirations and efforts so as to avoid disappointments and frustrations, and facilitate optimal attainments. We can hope that progressive installations of fiber-optic cable networks will make such communications as to human insights and collaborations increasingly informative, cogent and helpful.

Applications to Child Training

However, the effectiveness of communications among members of diverse groups and societies will in the future depend on how well the members have been prepared for comprehension and concerted action, preferably since childhood. This involves the following considerations.

For several months before birth the central nervous system of the human embryo is sufficiently developed to be sensorially "aware" that every bodily need is instantly met—in effect, the fetus is a secure, semiconscious monarch in a perfect and subservient Nirvana. For a few months after delivery some efforts—restlessness, a summoning cry—may be required, but then (modifying Otto Rank's concept of the "birth trauma"), the mother or some surrogate fulfills the demand for sustenance, warmth or other want or comfort: the neonate is still, as consciousness expands, a dominant princeling in a compliant milieu.

But it is this almost absolute narcissism that must be penetrated if a child is to adapt to a world outside itself. Well within the first two years the toddler should learn that not all demands can be instantly satisfied, that other beings—mother, father, siblings—also exist, often with competing wants and requirements of their own. The child should come to accept that only certain patterns of transactions with these and other newly recognized persons bring favorable results, whereas other modes do not. Even a genetically impaired child can be taught that sulks, tantrums or destructiveness, although not punished by counterviolence, will be predictably deterred by a diminution rather than an increase of attention or indulgence—with parental love ever present, but rewards restored only for desired conduct. With parents and teachers collaborating, this essential instruction can be extended from the child's Head Start and kindergarten experiences to an award, two decades later, of a Harvard Ph.D. in Education.

Adolescent years present special problems for guidance: friendships should be merited, retained and not exploited; talents should be recognized, encouraged and developed, but not in ways that engender fantastic ambitions; competitive rankings in studies and in the arts are to be gracefully accepted, pending further efforts to produce increasingly favorable judgments. However, parents who proudly but unthinkingly hear their athletic offspring cheered in gymnasiums or stadiums should consult an orthopedist as to whether to let their still physically vulnerable early teenager engage in rough body-contact sports such as boxing, wrestling, hockey, soccer and, particularly, high school football.

Sexuality

Contrary to Freud's concept of an eight-year "latency period," children of both sexes develop intense libidinous interests long before puberty, and manifest them in exhibitionisms, intersex curiosities and explorations, and manipulations of their genitalia leading to masturbation. Parents should not be excessively reactive; punishments often increase erotic interests and activities, and warnings about the dire effects of masturbation may cause traumatic anxieties as to the supposed damage already done, and later disbelief in, and disregard of, parental edicts.

Modifications of sexual concerns and behavior are best produced by simple, empathetic explanations from the parent of the same sex about the nature of sexuality and its role in adult happiness; excessive sexual preoccupations may be diminished by removing suggestive or frankly pornographic books, magazines and videotapes from ready availability, substituting judiciously regulated family TV viewing and, of course, cultivating more productive and satisfying interests, talents and activities.

Nevertheless, adolescents, even from parentally and economically stable homes, may present difficult problems. They now have ready extrafamilial access to erotic readings, songs and movies, experiments with disinhibiting drugs, and attendance at coeducational schools where teachers lecture "informingly"—in effect, often enticingly—about sexuality, and where class leaders of both sexes as young as thirteen boast competitively of fantasied or actual sexual conquests. Result: By age sixteen, six of ten male youngsters and four of ten girls have had coital experiences, often with traumatic anxieties, disillusionments, depressions and reactive intersex hostilities. When these are redirected toward negligent or contributory adults, there may be a virtual pandemic of allegations against teachers, coaches and other mentors who have had disturbed children and adolescents entrusted to them (Chapter 8).

Parental Reactions to Sexual Problems

These depend on many contingencies: the parents' cultural and religious convictions; their rapport with each other, with the troubled child or adolescent and with the school authorities involved; the family's economic and social status; and the nature and extent of previous difficulties involving any alleged moral or legal transgressions by the child. Far from least important, is the significance the parents attach to sociologic studies of sexuality among juveniles and alleged assaults on them by peers or adults.

Promiscuity. The data indicate that, contrary to widely held notions, there is no valid evidence that erotic explorations in childhood or coital experiences in adolescence impair later sexual and marital adaptations, provided those events have not been experienced as traumatic. In Indonesia there are many stable societies in which children have almost complete sexual freedom of action; in the West, Scandinavian parents may encourage adolescent sons to have mistresses as a way of selecting one of them or some other girl to wed, and elsewhere the great majority of married couples, as well as contented bachelor men and women, can unabashedly recall highly satisfactory sexual adventures beginning soon after puberty.

Allegations of Abuse. Even more difficult for troubled parents to acknowledge is that their child's charges may arise from a current custom among inadequately trained and experienced teachers and counselors literally to urge school children variously disturbed for other reasons to attribute their difficulties to sexual molestations by school staff or supervisory personnel. In some schools, open assemblies have been held in which such children have competed in presenting the most lurid accusations, usually directed against instructors who gave poor grades or denied them desired privileges.

It is well here to recall that, as described in Chapter 7, witches were hanged in New England after such an epidemic of charges made by delinquent girls, and that, currently, in some communities victims of false accusations are engaging in joint actions against school counselors or other professionals who elicit such allegations by intensely suggestive inquiries (Chapter 6). Parents should therefore be especially guarded in investigating their children's stories and their underlying motivations before initiating prosecution and taking reparative measures. In case of demonstrably false accusations, action may include persuading the child and its intended victim that a quiet withdrawal of the charge with a due apology would be in the best interests of all concerned.

Sexual Transgression. If a child has actually been assaulted, parental reactions should be even more circumspect, intelligent and forethoughtful. Clinical studies since the classical report by Karl Bowman, President of the American Psychiatric Association many years ago, have confirmed his conclusion that a child or adolescent may be less deeply and enduringly disturbed by the sexual experience than by the trauma of prolonged police questionings, cross-examinations at trials, press and TV publicity, emotionally charged environments at home and in school, and in residual situations thereafter. Therefore, while the sex offender is being arraigned, the parents and the prosecuting attorney should cooperate in keeping the child's depositions as gentle as possible, confining questioning by opposing lawyers to the judge's chambers with reporters excluded, controlling publicity insofar as possible, changing schools if advisable and diminishing tensions at home and elsewhere as indicated below.

Therapy. To be successful, the treatment of a troubled child (or adult), however traumatized, requires a restoration or enhancement of familial rapport, to be secured by reexplorations and resolutions of misunderstandings and consistent manifestations of reciprocated trust, care, confidence and concordant purposes. If parents and child are sincere, professional aid is usually not necessary but, if sought, the qualifications of projected consultants should be checked in their listings in specialty directories available in public libraries, and further selected in accord with the recommendations of the family physician or the advice of experienced friends; if this is not done, the child may be subjected to unneeded medications and hospitalizations, or to unnecessarily prolonged therapies, sometimes involving the family as co-patient rather than as cotherapist. When a professional is employed, his or her modalities of treatment should be coordinated with family guidance, but if such joint efforts do not produce favorable results within a reasonable period of a few weeks, additional consultation should be considered.

Sequential Sexual Guidance

As modified by the contingencies outlined above, the general principles to be followed at various ages are here summarized:

Preteen. Normal autoerotic and transsexual curiosities, if met with reproof and punishment, will become more secretive, intensive and emotionally disturbing. Early, simple explanations of their role in normal growth by the parent of the same sex, control of pornographic magazines and home video viewing, and encouragement of budding interest and participation in games, school studies and hobbies, and in the development of special talents in handiwork, painting, music or other artistic pursuits will open new outlets for emergent drives.

It may be well here to repeat that there is no evidence, other than questionably elicited case citations, for a current notion that abused children become abusive adults; there are no control studies of how many abused children grow up to be devoted parents and leaders of movements against misconceptions of child abuse.

Adolescence. Unless parents insist that their offspring remain celibate or virgin until marriage, their preteen instructions in sexuality may be extended as follows.

Boys may be cautioned, again preferably by their fathers, that in nearly every school and neighborhood there are girls targeted as "easy marks," "pushovers" or in some other derogatory jargon, but it is precisely such girls that are likely to transmit venereal diseases and/or to get pregnant and retarget the youngster being warned, with demands for financial support of mother and child. Additional caveat: Condoms are *not* sure protection against either eventuality. Further advice may include cautions that over-energetic "necking" and other bodily explorations (usually euphemized as lovemaking), especially with self-proclaimed virgins, may lead to accusations of sexual assault, with equally unpleasant consequences for the alleged transgressor and his family.

Alternative: A steady, mutually affectionate relationship with one girl of compatible interests. This may sometimes lead to jealousies, resentments, quarrels and depressions, but the teenager can be told that these reactions will probably recur and may become more intense in later affairs, but will then fade and end with a properly selected marital partner.

Girls—a few months before her daughter's expected menarche, a mother should explain the functions of menstruation in relation to sexuality and insemination. In view of the libidinal precocity of modern youth, this and later occasions present opportunities to discuss budding breasts, proper dress and demeanor, anticipated attentions from boys, appropriately responsive conduct, choice of boy and girl friends and, soon enough, the time, place, companionship, duration and monitoring of dates, the limits of exploratory "petting," and the very serious dangers of infection and pregnancy attendant on any genital contacts, however supposedly "protected." All communications should be in explicit terms, but sufficiently empathetic so that the daughter will not return with plaints such as: "But then I don't get dates," "I really love Harry," or "all the other girls do it"—all indicating that the troubled adolescent may try her own solutions for her problems, including secret abortion, dramatic suicide attempts, or teenage motherhood. No one can overemphasize the need for parental care, concern and foresighted wisdom in our current culture.

Relevance of Sexual Counseling

The paragraphs above were written to keep their contents within the theme of this book, but with the full knowledge that the sexual problems of our progeny are only a part of the far larger issues of school dropouts, vagrancy, drugs, lawless gangs, crime and related delinquencies. Further, these phenomena occur in the adverse environments provided for many of our youth: poor health care, inadequate education, racial and class enmities, economic instabilities, unemployment, corrupt and irresponsible governments and even the still hovering phantom of nuclear destruction.

I have dealt in greater detail with the related extensions of youthful guidance in the book *Adolescent Sexuality,* published in 1991 by Charles C. Thomas. However, until we can impart incremental wisdom as to how to establish an equitable, just and truly civilized world order in guiding our children, we adults must counsel the interim synthesis also discussed above:

Most of us will try to help you utilize your strengths, intelligence and talents toward the best attainments in life, but you must modify your ambitions so as to avoid deterrent frustrations and destructive individual and group reactions. This counsel arises from our failures to heed it and our hope that we have contributed to the foresight and progress you and your progeny will make toward global welfare in which sexuality—idealized as procreative and unifying "love"—will ever be essential.

Keynote Chord

Sexuality, when perverted by envy, jealousy, greed, vengeance or violence, can eventuate in severe social disruptions, and when devoted to false idols it can cause mass tragedies. Conversely, sublimated as mutual empathy, affection, care and service, and combined with other yearnings for creativity and existential transcendence, sexuality well serves mankind's slow and irregular, but historically demonstrable, progress toward a global civilization.

As philosopher Georg Hegel has dialectically assured us, "Thus also spake Zarathustra" to Persian youth six hundred years before Christ. But youth soon—all too soon—gives way to stultifying aging; hence, for young and old, Part Three of this book.

PART THREE

Youth and Age

Chapter 11

An Odyssey Extended

Chapter 1 began with a traumatic event that continues to affect the rest of my life. The present chapter will deal with many preceding experiences, all related to their social milieu and all affecting subsequent reactions. Readers may therefore be personally interested in parallel determinants in their own lives, such as early poverty, a recourse to study, work and music, the difficulties encountered in professional training, the intervening specter of premature death, later strivings for originality in thought, research, teaching and writing, the inner politics of universities and scientific societies, the fleeting auras of authorship and authority in contrast to the deep and lasting satisfaction secured by enduring friendships and, most of all, in an ideal marriage—now in its fifty-first year.

Thus the individual in his or her society, and so a return to personal narrative.

Genesis

I, Jules Masserman, was born in Chudnov, a village in old Russia near Kiev where those not of Slavic descent and of the Orthodox faith lived precariously. When I was three years old, my father left to seek dignity and freedom in mythical America, and two years later summoned my mother to bring my baby brother and me to join him there.

I barely remember being feverishly ill in the dark, fetid hold of a commercial freighter en route to Ellis Island, my mother's desperate pleas to an angelic immigration doctor who, through effective emergency action, prevented all of us from being sent back as bearers of some incurable disease, and the equally kindly official who then shepherded us, roped luggage and all, through bewildering immigrant catacombs to a train headed for what my mother thought was another rural hamlet called Detroit. There we lived in three rooms above my father's tailor shop until, aided economically by mother's earnings as a skilled seamstress, we moved to a home near an elementary school.

At the legally minimum age of thirteen, I obtained after-school and weekend employment in a drugstore. As my training and capacities permitted, I continued to add to the family finances and to my savings for a long envisaged medical education, by teaching violin, and by managing drugstores as a registered pharmacist during school vacations.

Sexuality. There is little to evade, conceal or confess. I recall no "Oedipus complex" troubling childhood (nor could I later discover one in three years of psychoanalysis). I experienced the normal libidinal awakenings during the so-called "latent" (i.e., preteen) period, and the usual yearnings and fantasies of adolescence, but home studies, music lessons, week-end work schedules, an unspoken but specific familial code and the generally prohibitive behavioral precepts for the young of that day left little opportunity for overt sexuality. An initial liaison in junior college with a young lady who proudly proclaimed herself a "freethinker," terminated when she informed me that she was also going to emancipate herself from me for other adventures, leaving me disillusioned and inactive until my courtship of gentle Jean during medical school.

Medical Education

I have described the intensive strains and satisfactions of these years in an earlier book called *A Psychiatric Odyssey;* here we can proceed to a more directly relevant account of my entry into medicine. The enrollment procedures at the Detroit College of Medicine are memorable: along with instructions to purchase dissecting tools, textbooks, a microscope and assorted paraphernalia, we were informed that intensive study and utmost diligence would be required and that, even so, little more than half the entering class could hope to graduate.

The ensuing year justified that warning: in Osteology we studied bare bones but with little reference to their role in motility, in Gross Anatomy we dissected arteries, veins, nerves, muscles and organs without an integrative grasp of their functions, in Embryology we peered at microscopic slides of chicken ova, and in Physiology we heard lectures which, as I discovered, had been cribbed from a British text published twelve years previously. Notebooks were submitted, dissections displayed, and many exams passed, but during the year about a quarter of the class dropped out.

Fortunately, the more highly motivated students had supplemented their instruction by extensive reading, and were better prepared for the second year courses in neurology, hematology, pathology and other preclinical medical orientations. However, my return as a sophomore courted disaster. Eight years of unremitting work and intensive study had taken their toll in a progressive physical exhaustion, now complicated by back pains and urinary difficulties. Cystoscopic and laboratory examinations revealed that both kidneys were tubercular, and indicated that I had less than a year to live unless the most seriously infected one was removed. This was done, and I recovered sufficient vitality to complete, with faculty indulgence, the remaining two months of my sophomore year. But then a very kindly Dean of Students called me into conference and spoke unforgettably as follows:

> My eager but foolish young friend, in view of your student record here it seemed possible that someday you would present a Graduation Address to your class; however, that would be seriously interfered with by your interim demise. The faculty has, therefore, decided that you must take a year or more off to recover your health. I, too, am sorry that there is no reasonable alternative, but I shall then guarantee your reentry for your final two years of clinical training.

Since there was no choice, I spent several weeks at bed rest under the directives of a visiting nurse and my mother's constant care. Soon I was able to resume teaching violin and viola and preparing for my return to medical school by studying a collection of borrowed clinical books and journals, and writing an essay on "Recent Renal Research" which won the 1927 Alpha Omega Alpha National Medical Student Award. I returned to school, graduated with median honors and secured an internship at the San Diego General Hospital where, in a favorable climate, my still draining postoperative wound finally healed.

Graduate Training

West and East Coasts. This consisted of a residency in neurology at Stanford, followed by three years as chief resident in psychiatry at the Baltimore City Hospitals where I conducted and published research on cerebral physiology. Most deeply appreciated were my concurrent studies at the famous Phipps Psychiatric Clinic at Johns Hopkins, headed by Adolf Meyer—then the acknowledged dean of American psychiatry. It was at Phipps that I learned how to integrate the genetic, somatic, unique experiential and concurrent sociocultural determinants of human conduct and how best to apply various therapeutic methods to modify an individual's social maladaptations, which, when disapproved, we often label and mistreat as neuroses and psychoses.

Chicago. On Dr. Meyer's recommendation, Roy Grinker, a Professor of Neurology at the University of Chicago, visited Phipps and invited me to help him initiate a new Department of Psychiatry. I accepted and in June, 1936, I was also awarded a Rockefeller Fellowship for four years of training at the Chicago Psychoanalytic Institute, including a personal analysis by its renowned director, Franz Alexander. At Chicago I also secured federal grants for a decade of comparative animal and clinical studies that led to the formulation of five Principles of Behavior, here condensed as follows.

Motivation. All higher animate behavior is actuated variably by emergent or predominant physiologic needs: respiration, nutrition, motility, milieu adaptation, sexual surcease, parental care and—for species survival—individual demise.

Perception. Higher organisms, including human, respond not to "absolute reality," but rather to their interpretation of their environment as determined by their genetic capacities and individual experiences.

Versatility. Most organisms can adapt to moderate frustration of a need either by evolving more effective ways of gratifying it, or by substituting satisfactions of other needs.

Deviance. However, when the required techniques exceed an organism's coping capacities, it develops somatic dysfunctions, sensed in humans as anxiety, spreading fears (phobias), ritualized compulsions for control, and other behavioral aberrations, including depressive, paranoid and even suicidal manifestations analogous to clinical neuroses and psychoses.

Therapeutics. Correspondingly, such reactions, when not entrenched and excessively self-destructive, can be alleviated or reversed by removal of stress, physiologic support, guided readaptations and the restoration of group relationships as most elaborately developed in human therapies.

Alcohol. Relevant to the last two principles were studies on the effects of various drugs, particularly, because of their clinical abuse, barbiturates and alcohol. In the latter case my associates and I subjected Vervet monkeys to a behavioral impasse between hunger and fear of a small (plastic) snake they had unexpectedly found in their food box. Predictably, they developed feeding inhibitions, immobile stupors, spreading phobias, depressive reactions, group isolations and other aberrations outlined in Principle Four above. Small quantities of alcohol in their milk disorganized and alleviated these complex aversions and restored the occasional intake of solid food, but the animals, given a choice, continued to prefer alcoholic drinks to the detriment of their nutrition; i.e., had become "alcohol addicts." These experiments were repeated, confirmed and recorded on a color-and-sound teaching film at the University of Vienna, and illustrated in a cartoon booklet distributed by the Canadian government in a campaign against the abuse of alcohol as an escape from anxiety.

By this time my studies, as published in my first book entitled *Behavior and Neurosis,* had become fairly widely appreciated; indeed, their human significance was featured in an illustrated article in the June 8, 1942, issue of *Time* Magazine.[Appendix, Reference 11] However, the comparative studies of addiction provoked a flood of letters asserting that alcoholism was blamelessly hereditary in humans, and that, on pain of unspecified retribution, I should instantly stop inducing or curing it in innocent animals.

Marriage

However, my greatest achievement at the University of Chicago was only incidentally academic. I had been leading an intensive but lonesome life; a gentle, shy, grade school teacher I had married during medical school had died of a rapidly spreading cancer, and a second marriage to a social worker at the university, unwisely contracted during my psychoanalysis, had terminated after only a few months. Two years later, at an interdepartmental meeting, I met Christine McGuire, an instructor in economics. Attracted by her grace and wisdom, I ventured to ask her to come sailing with me, and on the following Sunday we left the harbor in my aged wooden yawl. All went well for about an hour until one of the season's unpredictable squalls attacked Lake Michigan with low scudding dark clouds, rain and forty-knot winds. Waves rose, sails tore, the motor (predictably) quit and it was all I could do to regain the harbor and tie to a mooring. Whereupon Christine, whose previous boating experience had apparently been limited to cocktail hours on motor cruisers, remarked serenely: "I never imagined sailing could be such fun." Other dates followed—more sailing, concerts, plays, picnics, meetings with her parents and, on February 20, 1943, Christine and I were married in the beautiful Hilton Memorial Chapel of the University Theological School. She is now world renowned as an author and lecturer on medical education, and I, at age eighty-nine, am more convinced than ever that she is the most intelligent, loyal, helpful and altogether lovable person I shall ever know.

Academic and Other Developments

Three years after our marriage Christine and I became increasingly dissatisfied with the University of Chicago under the quasi-medieval regime of Chancellor Robert Maynard Hutchins and his Thomistic alter ego, Mortimer Adler. As but one example of its repressive scholasticism, in an article on "Psychiatry, Religion and Science" I had wondered whimsically whether any author of one of the "Hundred Great Books," exclusively designated "classics," would have wished to be associated with more than three of the others. Whereupon Professor Adler, in a published response, contended that with regard to history, literature and philosophy I was "manifestly schizoid"—an ex cathedra epithet for which he later had to apologize publicly.

Following other such symbolic experiences Christine welcomed an appointment in the Office of Research in Medical Education at the University of Illinois, where she rapidly advanced to Associate Director and earned international awards for her evaluation studies. Concurrently, I accepted a tenured Associate Professorship of Neurology and Psychiatry at Northwestern University. There, horizons broadened and life became ever more adventurous. Briefly recalled:

Research. I was provided with a well-equipped laboratory and trained assistants for further comparative behavioral studies. Results: many research reports and a book, *The Biodynamic Roots of Human Behavior,* that traced the evolution of animate conduct, and another volume, *Principles of Dynamic Psychiatry,* that further coordinated comparative and clinical studies and inferences.

Teaching. Highly qualified faculty personnel in psychiatry, psychology and social work at five university hospitals afforded excellent opportunities for initiating and evaluating interdisciplinary training of students and residents in their respective disciplines. I cherish a file of correspondence with Northwestern graduates, many of whom are now heads of departments at various universities.

Clinical. My academic arrangements with Northwestern allowed me to conduct a private practice. In this respect, my training and experience at Stanford, at Johns Hopkins, at the Psychoanalytic Institute and at the University of Chicago enabled me to discern and apply the following basic principles of human behavior.

Causation. Human travails arise primarily from the frustration of one or more of three universal and urgent ("Ur") needs: for physical vitality, for interpersonal securities, and for transcendent faiths essential to serenity (Chapter 9).

Therapy (Latin, *therapeien,* service). Treatment should serve to alleviate frustration of, or conflicts among, these needs and to guide the patient toward adequate satisfactions. Practically, treatment should utilize the following parameters here alliteratively summarized:

The *reputation* of the therapist not only as an expert in treating physical ills but also as a potential friend and empathetic spiritual mentor brings the patient (Latin, *patiens,* sufferer) for aid.

Introductory sessions then reassuringly clarify the therapist's interrelated roles, after which *rapport* is further enhanced by guided diminution of the patient's environmental and social stresses, supplemented when indicated by medications or other measures for the relief of anxiety, restlessness, depression or other psychosomatic reactions.

An illuminating biographic *review* of the traumatic experiences in the patient's childhood or later life that may have oversensitized him or her to current adversities will help to elicit corrective insights.

These *reorientations* as to more realistic adaptations to actual or imagined frustrations contribute to greater flexibility and appropriateness in interpersonal appraisals.

More broadly, these lead to *reconstructive* patterns of sociocultural behavior.

As necessary, therapy enhances these *re-adaptations* until reasonably satisfactory physical, cultural and existential Ur-goals are obtained not only for the patient, but also for the society in which he must live.*

In over a quarter century at Northwestern University and at

---

* Elaborated in *Principles of Dynamic Psychiatry* and *Practice of Dynamic Psychiatry,* both published by the W.B. Saunders Company.

my private office I treated hundreds of patients in accord with the medical, sociocultural and existential principles outlined above. As in all human endeavors, there were occasional disappointments, but among my most valued possessions are letters from former patients and students, many now prominent in business, scientific, organizational and political fields, expressing gratitude for their therapy and their subsequent accomplishments.

The Center for the Advanced Study of the Behavioral Sciences. In 1968 I was appointed Honorary Fellow in Psychiatry at this Olympian institution and there, except for a month as Visiting Professor at Australian and New Zealand universities, spent my term in integrative studies with other Fellows in genetics, anthropology, biology, history, sociology, mathematics and philosophy—disciplines I found remarkably relevant to psychiatry. In appreciation, I wrote *A Psychiatric Odyssey,* an interim autobiography intended for other seekers for comprehensive enlightenment, which must always remain pitifully incomplete. Its Preface can be briefly paraphrased:

> Here in my Center sanctum high above San Francisco Bay I sit listening to Mozart's deeply introspective String Quintet Opus 516 in perfect counterpoint to my own reflections. Can this *Odyssey* ever empathetically convey my own troubled and ever-partial transitions from reader to understander, from experimenter to researcher, from schoolman to scholar, from physiologist to physician? Yet should I not try to emulate the autobiographic accounts of the many historic and current mentors—from Aristotle through Maimonides and Spinoza to Freud, Schweitzer and Adolf Meyer—who have inspired me? Here, then, my own efforts to communicate with fellow Odyssiasts.

Travel. My university schedule was compatible with other prolonged periods away for invited lectures at medical schools and to professional societies in South America, Europe, the former USSR, Egypt, Israel, China, India, Japan and Australia. Christine was also usually invited and also spoke on her interests—often so effectively as to put me in the role of being addressed as Mr. McGuire by many in her audience.

Advancement. I progressed from Associate Professor to Co-chairman of Neuropsychiatry at Northwestern University, where I served until mandatory retirement at age sixty-seven. Dr. Harold Visotsky, with organizational and administrative genius, then expanded the department into a local Division of Behavioral Sciences that has attained national renown.

Awards. These included the prestigious 1964 Albert Lasker Award for "Outstanding Contributions to the Advancement of Mental Hygiene," the Sigmund Freud Award in 1974, the 1977 Taylor Manor Award for Psychiatrist of the Year, the Veterans Affairs Award for Outstanding Educator in 1978, and many others from universities and professional societies.

Organizations. I helped found the International Association of Social Psychiatry and later organized its American Regional Society, participated in launching the American Academy of Psychoanalysis and was elected president of all three. I was also elected simultaneously or successively president of the American Society for Group Therapy, of the American Society for Biological Psychiatry and, in 1978-79, of the American Psychiatric Association. With regard to the incredible denouement to the latter (Chapters 3 and 4), on October 26, 1993, I received the certified letter reproduced on page *xv*, absolving me of all charges of unethical or unprofessional conduct. I replied in kind (page *xvi*). I have, nevertheless, withdrawn from most organizational activities other than as Honorary Life President of the World Association for Social Psychiatry and as President of the Foundation for International Accords.

Philosophical

Reflecting on the past decade, Christine and I feel that we have surmounted the pain and bitterness of a series of injustices and, in writing this book, have contributed to an understanding and possible amelioration of a pervasive problem of our time.

Coda: Existential

For half a century I have been privileged to visit and learn much about the customs, literatures and philosophies of many cultures, to hear their fascinating music and to stand in awe of their masterpieces in painting, sculpture and architecture. With what wisdom I could gather, I have authored or edited scores of books and hundreds of articles, been awarded various honors and been accorded many friendships and a cherished marital love.

Why then, still a remnant of a restlessness and seeking? I have read that this question was posed by Pharaoh Djoser to his vizier Imhotep, by the Sphinx in classical Greece, and by philosophers and poets ever since—and has yet to be answered. Perhaps an eternal search for the unknown and transcendent is part of life itself. Having long ago—I am now in my ninetieth year[Appendix, Reference 12]—conceded that omniscience is neither possible nor necessary and that erudition is best applied in action, my compromises are these:

Deep appreciation of a long and full life

Retention of sincere friendships here and abroad through correspondence, visits when practical and mutual services

Continuation of interests in literature, the arts and sciences

Creative writing and composing

And most of all, serenity in an ideal marital companionship

May providence grant our readers similar satisfactions throughout their lives.

EPILOGUE
Justice Repossessed

Barbara W. Stackler

The human condition is a contradiction in terms. We go about our business of living with a wary and cynical eye, hoping that fate will not deal us an unforeseen and unkind blow. However, we also have an inherent need to trust. It is that trust that is the chink in our armor, making us vulnerable to destruction by those who seek to use and exploit us. When confronted with these destructive forces, our mettle is tested. The weak fall, and only the strong prevail and are victorious.

The foregoing true story is one of victory. In all respects, it is a story of the triumph of the human will and spirit over overwhelming adversity. This hard-won victory belongs to Jules and Christine Masserman and not to Barbara Noel and her ilk. As instigator and zealous exploiter of the events recounted here, she was merely the catalyst that tested the true mettle of the Massermans.

In September of 1984, Barbara Noel accused Dr. Jules Masserman of rape. Only Barbara Noel knows her true motive. Therefore, permit me to speculate.

Jules Masserman was seventy-nine years old at the time of Ms. Noel's accusations. At that time, Barbara Noel had been

Dr. Masserman's patient for more than eighteen years. She was under his care because of severe psychological problems associated with a failed personal life and failing career as a singer and songwriter. She revealed that she had been sexually abused by her father. She was an alcoholic and substance abuser. She had financial problems. She was and is an "exploiter" of others.

Dr. Jules Masserman, on the other hand, had achieved all the things Barbara Noel sought: international fame as a distinguished psychiatrist, lecturer and teacher, a happy marriage, and financial security.

Like an Ayn Randian pariah, it occurred to Ms. Noel that the fame and fortune she so desperately sought could be gained vicariously. She must attack and destroy one with celebrity. Why not exploit the celebrity of Jules Masserman? This idea is nothing new. How better to achieve fame than to murder Caesar? So began the events described in this book.

Barbara Noel has spent most of the last decade promoting her ludicrous tale. Most recently it has been fodder for a book and a film. With each telling, the story grows "larger" and more incredible, like Pinocchio's nose.

I am happy to report that despite Barbara Noel's unholy assault, Jules Masserman and his extraordinary spouse of over fifty years, Christine, have prevailed. They continue to flourish in both their professional and personal lives. Jules Masserman, at the advanced age of eighty-nine, continues to make significant contributions to the betterment of mankind. It is clear that the bizarre experience recounted in this book has strengthened rather than diminished him.

Jules and Christine continue to affirm the strength and resiliency of the human spirit. Their story should serve as a beacon to all civilized persons. I confess that I am an unabashed admirer. In addition to serving as their counsel, I am honored to be counted among their legion of friends.

Appendix*

* Documents quoted in full or nearly so in the text are not here duplicated.

Reference 1

Sodium Amytal

The employment of amytal interviews during crises in Ms. Noel's comprehensive treatment was described in Chapters 1 and 4; this Reference reviews their rationale and application in other branches of medicine and law.

Amytal (chemically, amobarbitol sodium) interviews have been usefully employed in neuropsychiatric therapy for three quarters of a century, and were fully described by the author in his *Practice of Dynamic Psychiatry* (W.B. Saunders Press), Lawrence Wolberg's *Techniques of Psychotherapy* (Intercontinental Press), the American Psychiatric Association's *The Psychiatric Therapies* (APA Press) and the *Comprehensive Textbook of Psychiatry* by Kaplan, Freedman and Sadock (Williams and Wilkins Press). Among its many advantageous applications in intravenous solution are the following.

Medical. In doses of around 500 mg. (less active material than in two tablets of aspirin), amytal can control an epileptic seizure, can alleviate obsessive agitations (such as in physically unhurt but mentally traumatized combat personnel) and is useful as a quietly reassuring preliminary to surgical anesthesia.

Forensic. Accused persons, plaintiffs, defendants and witnesses in criminal or tort suits may, with their fully informed and written consent, agree to have their testimony under amytal sedation electronically recorded while being questioned by opposing attorneys or police officials. However, *since such testimony, even if duly sworn and directly reproduced, may demonstrably represent merely disinhibited motivations, altered* *memories or wishful fantasies, it is not admissible in court.* Nevertheless, it may still offer valuable clues as to facts or illusions to be confirmed by incontestable modes of examination.

As a consultant to the Chicago Police Department, I employed amytal interviews to aid the defense of a school official accused of child abuse, to clear a police officer of charges of unnecessarily wounding and, thereby, disabling a fleeing robbery suspect, who was later convicted and, conversely, expediting the arrest of a suspected embezzler, also later convicted. However, in this Heisenbergian era of ever certain uncertainty, I cannot assert that justice was always achieved in these and other cases, all of which must be held confidential as to identifying details.

Therapeutic. Amytal interviews, if employed at all, should be part of a comprehensive program of therapy, with empathetic, skillfully directed analysis of the patient's genetic proclivities, experiential moldings, attendant anxieties and sensitivities, and his or her compensatory attainments and aspirations. The agenda may include conjoint marital counseling, helpfully directive educational, occupational and group orientation, and other modes of integrative treatment leading to progressive improvements in the patient's personal, occupational and social adaptations. All of these provisions were followed in Ms. Noel's therapy as described in Chapters 1 and 4.

Reference 2

Evidence from Ms. Noel's Gynecologist

The following are the attested Office Notes of Dr. Stuart Abel, Ms. Noel's gynecologist, regarding her office visit of September 21, 1984.

Note the marginal indication in Dr. Abel's record which quotes Ms. Noel as follows:

> Says she was either raped or dreamt she was raped while under the influence of amytal in her psychiatrist's office. Wanted me to tell her.

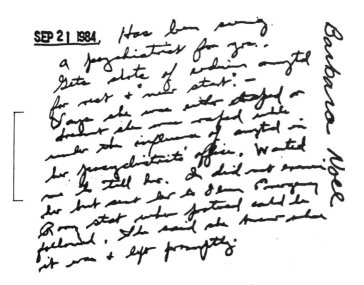

Reference 3

Evidence from Ms. Noel's Internist

The following are the attested Office Notes of Dr. Coleman Seskind, Ms. Noel's internist, regarding her office visit of September 21, 1984.

Note the marginal indication in Dr. Seskind's record that Ms. Noel "wonders whether she has been hallucinating."

3-84 Chest – Calcified [illegible] glands, slight ↑ in lung markings in both mid + lower lung fields . . .

12/5/84

SEP 21 1984 went to clinic 3x Wonders about recent [illegible]

POF ↓ 4 got worried, whether she has been hallucinating

[illegible] saw Dr. Mazzone – 1966

[illegible] lotion – smell – 7 yrs ago

Talk to See Dr. Stewart Abel

110/50 666 [illegible] LSD 787-8613

P [illegible]

9/24/84 went to [illegible] ER

[illegible] "[illegible]" – [illegible] test at urine lab – [illegible] said – results [illegible]

Vag fluid –

10/5/84 No evidence of rape [illegible] – saw – 2 lawyers – one wants to see no evidence

Saw Dr. Hefter X3

got [illegible] for V.D [illegible]

VDRL negative

NOV 02 1984 – late cancellation

NOV 05 1984 frightened to come to bldg – began to [illegible] – dazed.

124 # Dr. Mazzone called her – reference to atty

Civil suit filed – 10/4

SEPT 22.0 (5-55.0) [illegible] Manuel Silberman – 800 [illegible] psychologist 1X Clozol

VDRL [illegible] 110/60 to see him [illegible] Present [illegible]

City Hall – negative 10 yrs. [illegible] – Dr.

Reference 4

Report of Police Officer Fleming

The following is the attested official report made by Officer Fleming, the police officer who immediately investigated the Noel complaint on the afternoon of September 21, 1984.

Note the marginal indication on the second page of Officer Fleming's report, which quotes Ms. Noel as follows:

"VICTIM STATED TO R/O* THAT SHE WAS UNABLE TO DETERMINE WHETHER INCIDENT WAS A DREAM OR REALITY."

*Responding Officer

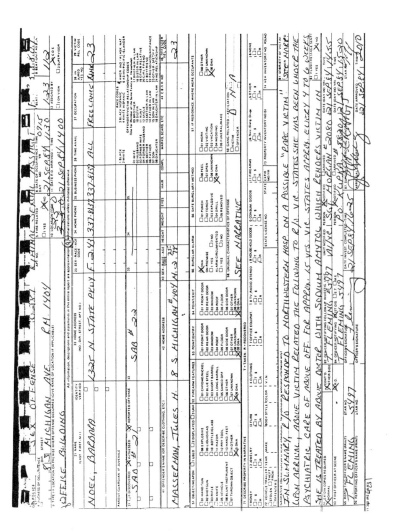

THE VICTIM SCHULZ STATE FOR APPEAR. BY HER, ASKED IF SHE WOULD LIKE 3-3-81 OR

VICTIM STATES ON TODAY'S DATE SHE HAD ANTO REMAIN IN OFFICE FOR AWHILE TO GET DRUG

APPOINTMENT WITH OFF. AT DAS HES. AND WAS WEAR OFF AND VIC STATED "YES" OFF. THEN

TREATED WITH SODIUM AMYTAL. VICTIM STATES LEFT ROOM AND VIC. GOT UP AND DRESSED,

WHEN SHE AWOKE FROM DRUG SHE FELT WENT INTO OFF.'S OFFICE AND SAID SHE FELT
VIC. STATES THERE WAS SEXUAL PENETRATION.
SOMEONE LAYING ON TOP OF HER VICTIM THEN DRUG WELL ENOUGH TO LEAVE. OFF. REQUESTED

HER EYES AND BODY BECAME RIGID. AT THIS TIME VIC. TO CALL HIS OFFICE WHEN SHE ARRIVED HOME,

OFF. GOT UP OFF OF VIC., WENT TO WASH BASIN VIC. STATES THIS WAS THE FIRST TIME OFF.

AND WASHED OFF, GOT DRESSED AND LEFT ROOM. MADE SUCH REQUEST. VIC. THEN LEFT OFFICE

VIC. STATES SHE HAD CLOSED HER EYES AT THIS AND PROCEEDED TO HOSPITAL. VICTIM STATED TO

POINT TO ACT AS IF SLEEPING AND APPARENTLY C/O THAT SHE WAS UNABLE TO DETERMINE WHETHER INCIDENT
WAS A DREAM OR REALITY. BY 4/3 ON SCENE. DET.
DOZED OFF FOR ONE HOUR OR TIME. VIC. NEXT KELLY #143 DAY DT 3/3/81 ON SCENE.

REMEMBERS OFF. RE-ENTERING ROOM AND AWAKENING

Reference 5

Evidence from
Emergency Room Physicians

The following is the attested record of Northwestern Memorial Hospital Emergency Room physicians' examination of Ms. Noel on September 21, 1984.

Note marginal indication in the record reporting no evidence of external trauma or assault.

PHYSICIAN'S COPY

Reference 6

Report of Detective Kelly

The following is the attested official report made by Detective Kelly, the police officer in charge of investigating the Noel case.

Note the marginal indication (page 3 of Report) that Ms. Noel did not want the allegation reported to Dr. Masserman because "there was a slight possibility that she dreamed the incident"...and that Detective Kelly recommends "that this case be EX-CLEARED."

Notes and descriptions of all property or evidence recovered at the end of the Narrative in column form. Show exactly where found, when found, who found it. Don't show quantity of each item. Inventory numbers. If property taken was secured for Operation Identification, indicate I.D. number at end of Narrative. Offender's approximate description, if possible, should include name, nickname, sex, race code, age, height, weight, color eyes & hair, complexion, scars, marks, etc. If suspect is arrested, give name, sex, race code, age, C.B. or I.R. number, if known, and state in Custody.

SUPPLEMENTARY REPORT	All descriptions and statements in this entire report are approximations or summarizations unless indicated otherwise.	4 DATE OF ORIG. OCCURRENCE – TIME

CHICAGO POLICE

1 OFFENSE-CLASSIFICATION LAST PREVIOUS REPORT	1 UCR OFF CODE	2 ADDRESS OF ORIG. INCIDENT/OFFENSE	1 VERIFIED	2 CORRECTED	3 BEAT OF OCC.
Criminal Sexual Assault	0281	8 S. Michigan Av. 1404			123

5 VICTIM'S NAME AS SHOWN ON CASE REPORT	CORRECT 1 YES 2 NO	IF NO, CORRECT ALL VICTIM INFORMATION IN BOXES 20 THROUGH 27	6 FIRE RELATED 1 YES 2 NO	7 BEAT/UNIT ASSIG.
Noel, Barbara				612

8 TYPE OF LOCATION OR PREMISE WHERE INCIDENT/OFFENSE OCCURRED	LOCATION CODE	9 NO. OF VICTIMS	10 NO. OF OFFENDERS
Office Building	250	1	1

Victim: Noel, Barbara F/w/43, 1325 N. State Parkway
                   Apt. 4C, 337-8139, Employed as a Freelance
                   Singer for TV Commercials

Offender: Masserman, Jules H. M/W/78, 8 S. Michigan,
                   Rm. 1404, 263-7343 - Psychiatrist

Injuries: None visible

Taken to: Northwestern Hospital - Dr. Marshall

Location: 8 S. Michigan, RM.1404

Date & Time: 21 Sep 84, 0915 - 1130 hrs.

90. EXTRA COPIES REQUIRED (NO. & RECIPIENT)	91. DATE THIS REPORT SUBMITTED	TIME	92. SUPERVISOR APPROVING (PRINT NAME)	STAR NO.
Normal	2 Oct 84	1900	Sgt. J. Murphy	1389
93 REPORTING OFFICER (PRINT NAME)	STAR NO.		SIGNATURE	
Det. J. Zelly	14364		J. Murphy	
		95 DATE APPROVED (DAY-MO.-YR) 2 OCT 84	TIME 2000	

*MUST BE COMPLETED IN ALL CASES

Page 2

Area 1 Violent Crimes

2 Oct 84
F-350609

Manner: The offender is the victim's psychiatrist and had victim under Sodium Amytal when he put his penis in her vagina.

Evidence: Vitullo Evidence Kit E.I. #13463
Inventory #125293 - Crime Lab

Personnel Assigned: Off. T. Fleming #5497, Beat 112
Det. J. Kelly #14364, Area 1 VC

Notifications: Dept. of Human Services

Witness/Outcry: Dr. Coleman Seskind M/w, 8 S. Michigan
Rm. 1206, 726-7595 - Victim's Physician

Investigation: On 21 Sep 84 at 1530 hrs. the undersigned was sent to the Northwestern Hospital on a Criminal Sexual Assault. Interviewed victim and she related the following basic facts but not verbatim. She has been under psychiatric care with Dr. Jules Masserman for the past 15 years. She sees him in his office every 4 to 6 weeks and is treated with Sodium Amytal and she is usually unconscious for approx. 3 to 4 hours. She related that he has her undress down to her panties before he puts her under. On several occassions in the past 15 years she would wake up and have a strong scent of Dr. Masserman's aftershave lotion on her shoulders but did not give it any thought. On one occassions she woke up and had bruises on her arm and he told her that she became violent while unconscious and he had to restrain her.

On 20 Sep 84 she had an appointment and Dr. Masserman called her and switched the appointment to 21 Sep 84. When she arrived on 21 Sep 84 she striped down to her panties and he administered the sodium amytal. At approx. 1130 hrs. she woke up and felt someone on top of her with his penis in her vagina. She became rigid and opened her eyes. She saw the offender get up and go to a wash basin in the room and wash himself. He then got dressed and left the room. She related that she closed her eyes to pretend she was sleeping and dozed off. She then remembers Dr. Masserman coming back into the room and waking her up. He wanted her to remain until the drug wore off and he left the room again. The victim then got dressed and told him she was leaving. Dr. Masserman asked her to call him when she got home and the victim said this was the first time he ever wanted her to call. The victim related that there is usually a woman receptionist present when she has a visit but on this date she was not present.

When the victim left his office she went to her Physician's office, Dr. Coleman Seskind, 8 S. Michigan, Rm. 1206, and told him that she believes the offender had raped her.

F 350609

Page 3

Area 1 Violent Crimes

2 Oct 84
r-550069

Dr. Leskind told her to go see her Gynecologist and she went to 680 N. Lake Shore Dr. and told Dr. Stuart Abel what had happened. He instructed her to go to the Northwestern Hospital for an examination. Hospital personnel contacted the police and Beat 112 responded and made the original report. A Vitullo Evidence Kit was prepared. Northwestern Hospital did a cursory examination of the slides and found no semen. The victim related that she does not believe that the offender had an orgasim.

The victim related that she did not want the offender confronted with the allegation because there was a slight possibility that she dreamed the incident while she was unconscious. She related that she was going to confer with her attorney.

On 27 Sep 84 the victim was recontacted and related that she has conferred with her attorney and she is not going to persue the matter criminally at this time. As the victim refuses to prosecute at this time request that this case be EX-CLEARED at this time.

Det. J. Kelly #14364
Area 1 Violent Crimes

-7 OCT 1984   05 07

Reference 7

APA President Hartmann's Letter

The following is the letter from then APA President Hartmann following the IPS-APA Ethics Committee hearings.

Note the marginal indication confirming the IPS-APA agreement not to publicize the Noel case.

November 8, 1991

Jules Masserman, M.D.
2231 East 67th Street
Chicago, IL 60649

RE: Ethics Review

Dear Jules:

Thanks for your letter about the Illinois and APA ethics proceedings.

As I hope you know, I am full of respect for you, have been for many years, and remain so – for you and your long, many-faceted, excellent, and creative career in psychiatry.

I am pained by the content of the Illinois and APA ethics hearings on your case, about which I have been informed from time to time because of many people's wish that I be satisfied that you be given both full due process and full respectful hearing. I do think you have been given full, fair hearing and due process and respect; and I do not want the APA Board to overrule or supersede full and fair process by adding an extraordinary level to what has been done.

I am glad the Illinois Psychiatric Society has decided not to publicize their decision in this case, as is their option with APA ethics review supervision.

I am sorry this process has caused you so much distress, but I hope that one area of distress does not unduly shadow your knowledge, and mine, that you have had many areas of great success and excellence over many years in psychiatry.

Best wishes,

Lawrence Hartmann, M.D.
President

Reference 8

Ann Landers' Communications

Herewith a letter from "Eppie" and the autograph from the complimentary copy of her *Encyclopedia* (page 166). Also, for the record, her three words of heartfelt sympathy for the falsely accused in her column of September 10, 1993.

In the *Chicago Tribune* of September 10, 1993, "Ann Landers" printed a letter from a man who, after being arrested and indicted on a malicious charge of rape, suffered great financial loss and months of personal agonies and social humiliations before proving the charge completely false and instituting countersuits to clear his name and obtain compensation. His letter concludes: "I have no doubt... there are many men in prison on rape convictions who are as innocent as I am. My heart goes out to all of them." Ms. Landers' heartfelt sentiment: "So does mine, but I'll bet an equal number... who are guilty... are... free as the breeze."

Ann Landers
Field Newspaper Syndicate
Chicago Sun-Times Building
Chicago, Illinois 60611

June 21, 1982

Jules H. Masserman, M.D.
8 South Michigan Avenue
Chicago, Illinois 60603

Dear Jules:

Thank you for your generous letter, along with
the superb resolution against nuclear war, which was
written by you.

I read it twice and can see why it was readily
adopted. No one has ever said it better.

Bless you for your leadership in this most vital
of all efforts. If we don't solve this one, there
won't be any others left to solve because there won't
be any people.

Fondest,

Eppie

EFL/cd

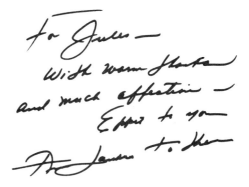

Reference 9

Retained Status in the APA— Scientific and Administrative

In a gracious Foreword to my book, *Writing and Editing the Humanities* (Amereon, 1992), John Nemiah, Editor-in-Chief of the *American Journal of Psychiatry,* wrote:

> There is perhaps no one better suited than Dr. Jules Masserman to be the Vergil for our *descensus Averno.* The author of many published scientific writings of his own, he has been an equally distinguished editor of the works of others during his half-century as investigator and scholar.... He has distilled that experience into helpful instructions for... working smoothly with publishers, and for maintaining tactful relationships with officers of organizations....
>
> Though modest in length, Dr. Masserman's treatise is long on the advice and wisdom it brings to all of us....

AMERICAN PSYCHIATRIC ASSOCIATION
1400 K STREET. N.W., WASHINGTON, D.C. 20005
Office of Membership

January 15, 1993

Jules H Masserman M.D.
2231 East 67th Street
Chicago IL 60649-1206

Dear Doctor Masserman:

I am pleased to have the opportunity to contact you at this time to express our appreciation for your 57 years of continued support of the Association. As a Life Fellow with 57 years of membership in the APA, you are relied upon to guide us on the important issues that affect the future of the profession and the quality of patient care.

Your membership card, validated for 1993, is attached in the tear-off section of this letter. If you should have any questions about your APA affiliation, please contact me or the Office of Membership at the above address.

I would like to take this opportunity to encourage you to attend the 146th Annual Meeting to be held in San Francisco, California, May 22-27, 1993. The scientific program will offer a wide variety of excellent continuing medical education sessions. The theme of this year's meeting, selected by our President, Dr. Joseph T. English, is "Patient Care for the 21st Century: Asserting Professional Values Within Economic Constraints." Many of the scientific sessions will focus on this important topic, including a special presidential symposium. You will be receiving the Advance Registration Information Packet this month and I hope you will send in your registration early. We hope to see you in San Francisco.

Your affiliation represents the Association's most important asset. I invite your comments, suggestions, and ideas that will enhance our ability to provide the best benefits and services in keeping with the overall goals of the APA and its membership.

Cordially,

Melvin Sabshin

Melvin Sabshin, M.D.
Medical Director

Reference 10

Child Abuse

What is considered child abuse depends on the times (see also Chapter 8).

In the early thirteenth century two fanatic leaders, each claiming divine direction, organized separate Children's Crusades to regain the Holy Land from its Muslim desecrators. Despite the concern of Pope Innocent III, none of the teenage crusaders reached Palestine; instead some twenty thousand were sold by European traders into prostitution and slavery in Africa. Nonetheless, the movement inspired the Sixth Crusade.

Reference 11

Early Recognition

The June 8, 1942, issue of *Time* Magazine reported on my comparative experimental and clinical research on the causes and cures of behavioral disorders in animals and humans.

MEDICINE

Torkel Korling
DR. MASSERMAN & SUBJECT
What makes & breaks a neurosis?

Catatonic Cats

For hours she sat in her corner, staring silently into space, her pupils dilated, her heart pounding, her breathing labored. She shunned her old friends, refused to eat for days at a time. Occasionally she became agitated or infantile and kittenish. But often she just sat, in a catatonic stupor, brooding and lonely, quiet as a cat.

In fact, she was a cat. She was a typical example of some 200 animals made neurotic by University of Chicago Psychoanalyst Jules H. Masserman in the last three years. His purpose in this scientific cat & mouse game: to find out by experiment what makes & breaks a neurosis. At the American Psychiatric Association meeting in Boston last fortnight Psychoanalyst Masserman presented his results, showed movies of the first animals in medical history who were first given nervous breakdowns, then cured of them by psychotherapy.

How To Go Crazy. Working on a grant from the Otho Sprague Institute, Dr. Masserman rigged up an automatic feeding apparatus which dropped some food into the feedbox of a glass cage every time a light flashed on. He then trained cats, one at a time, to lift the lid of the feedbox whenever the light flashed. After the cats were conditioned to associate light with food, he shot a harmless blast of air into the cage at the moment the cat reached for the lid. This gale at mealtime frightened the cats. After repeated frustrations the animals associated the feedbox and signal light with fear. Frustration and the conflict between hunger and fright drove the cats quietly mad.

Like human beings, they showed their psychic illnesses in many ways. They developed "anxiety neuroses," their fur stood on end, they crouched, they trembled. Some refused to eat, or became food faddists. Some became catatonic cats.

How to Get Sane. Dr. Masserman left the animals to their phobias and conflicts for several months, then set out to cure them by psychiatric sessions in the experimental cage. One group he treated by "reassurance and suggestion." The cats were gently carried to the feedbox, stroked and fondled, petted and coaxed to eat. At first, when the doctor stopped stroking, the cats stopped feeding. But gradually they lost their fears.

A second group he treated by a method often tried on pilots who have crashed. He made the cats "break through" their phobias by forcing them to eat, in much the same way that a cracked-up pilot is sometimes forced to fly again. Cats handled pilot-fashion not only overcame their fright but turned into daredevils, learned to enjoy blasts of air with their dinners.

Most unique cat therapy was a method employed in human psychoanalysis. Like a good psychoanalyst, Dr. Masserman quietly observed his patients as they "worked through" their own problems. They were given many opportunities to fiddle with the light switches and the lid of the box, learn for themselves what had produced their neuroses. Through repeated trials they gradually developed "insight" into the sequence of light switch, food, air blast, finally became well-adjusted, normal cats.

Concerning this striking evidence of psychotherapy's biological basis, Dr. Masserman cryptically notes at the end of his film: "Any similarity between these experiments and human behavior is purely coincidental[?]." On the cats' opinion of human behavior, Dr. Masserman said nothing.

Reference 12

Sexuality, Sense and Senescence

*Send not to know for whom the
bell tolls; it tolls for thee.*
— John Donne (1573-1651)

The young assume that they will never grow old, and the middle-aged assiduously deny or misinterpret the inevitable inroads of aging. But neither evasion can be long successful, and both diminish the capacities of the elderly to adapt to the stresses of advancing years, such as those recounted in this book. Moreover, unlike Maimonides, author of the famed twelfth-century *Guide To The Perplexed,* many of us in later life may become discouraged about the efficacy of imparting to the young any of the insights and precepts we ourselves acquired.

This final section is therefore devoted to modes of thought and action which, from the author's personal as well as clinical experience, may best meet the inevitable physical and psychologic impairments and existential concerns of aging, retain *élan vital* and, for our sake as well as theirs, conserve our capacity and dedication to counsel, guide and perhaps inspire future generations, as discussed in Chapter 10.

Sexuality

This is frequently of prime concern. Men after fifty often regard diminished libido and potency as dire omens of senility, and react in ways that may seriously trouble their lives. Adverse responses may include:

Trials of various erotogenic drugs (aphrodisiacs). Most are

suggestively advertised, expensive but physiologically inactive placebos (e.g., powdered rhinoceros horns, symbolic of erect phalluses); others may be dangerous. Among the latter: cantharides extracts are toxic to the urinary tract; pencil-like dildos inserted into the urethra damage its delicate lining; and even small doses of testicular extracts containing testosterone, a male hormone, may initiate a prostatic cancer.

Concurrently troublesome may be a search for "lost youth" through sexual adventures with young women, usually leading to emotional attachments, irrational jealousies, disappointments and, far too often, loss of a formerly devoted wife and family. Nor can the dangers of a recourse to prostitutes, with the attendant risks of venereal infections, police arrests and, as currently exploited, blackmail, be disregarded.

With such pitfalls avoided, relief from intercurrent anxieties and depressions can be secured without drugs, from assurances by physicians and trusted friends that, while libidinal urges normally abate, sexual pleasures can continue well into the ninth decade. Marital couples that have retained and enhanced their mutual affection need only some simple counseling as to more effectively stimulating foreplay in a variety of positions, a slowing and prolongation of coitus and, when indicated, its relaxed and satisfying termination without the necessity of an intensive orgasm. Detailed instructions are rarely required, but are readily available in manuals such as those by Masters and Johnson, purchasable at local bookstores. However, bachelor or widowed men who seek such reassuring experiences had best find them with women near their own age, since such companions, in the words of Benjamin Franklin, an historic authority in the field, are likely to be "more experienced, accommodating—and grateful."

Sensorial Concerns

While the somatic and psychologic impairments discussed below will affect sexual sensitivity and performance to varying degree, they are here considered with regard to their optimal adaptations in the interests of retained contentment and creativity in daily living.

Audition. Insidious impairments of hearing are at first projected externally: it seems that people do not speak as clearly as formerly, especially when conversing in groups in a noisy environment; telephone messages sound garbled; lectures from auditorium podiums become incomprehensible; violin virtuosos do not produce the rich, golden tones they formerly elicited from their instruments, and conductors of familiar symphonies seem to insist on unique interpretations ranging from deafening sforzandos to completely inaudible pianissimos.

Eventually, at the urging of family and friends, the deficiency is acknowledged and confirmed by elaborate audiometer tests and the prescription of individually fitted hearing aids. These amplify basic sounds, but do not correct for the especially diminished perception of the high-pitched tones characteristic of speech and music. A vaunted (and expensive) "technical miracle," digitally computerized to compensate each ear for treble loss, may then be purchased, but this requires carrying a pocketful of miniature batteries and a six-inch-long cylindrical "control tower" that must be frequently reset for changing environments. Concerts become somewhat more enjoyable, and the confused babel at cocktail parties more tolerable.

Vision. Diminished visual acuity is particularly stressful to artists, to artisans with refined skills and to professionals who must rely mainly on the printed word for progress in their specialties. Multifocal eyeglasses only partially correct near and far vision, and lens replacements for cataracts cannot influence astigmatic retinal irregularities or advancing macular degeneration. Bright lights, hand held magnifiers and telescopic attachments, available at various specialty stores, help, as do other devices on display at Low Vision Centers and the local offices of the Guild for the Visually Handicapped. In a highly commendable service, books and magazines recorded on audiotapes or plastic discs can be borrowed gratis from the Library of Congress or from its regional branches countrywide, thus expanding cultural interests and sources of reference for lectures and writing.

However, as vision slowly dims, pilot's licenses are not renewed, night driving must be especially cautious, travel requires a competent—and patient—companion, and other life patterns must be suitably modified. Nevertheless, in nearly all cases an empathetic ophthalmologist can offer assurances that debility will not reach the white-cane stage, and that life can continue actively, creatively and relatively happily.

Olfaction, Taste, Touch. These perceptions were developed early in animate evolution as signaling food, sex or danger, but are of relatively minor concern to aging humans other than gourmets or oenophiles. However, loss of tactile sensitivity slows reflexes and delicate manipulations in painting, modeling or similar hobbies.

Memory

An elderly person can readily and accurately recall names, dates, events and a multitude of obscure and esoteric data relevant to previous interests in literature, science, arts or sports—yet forget where he put his spectacles and keys four minutes ago, or worse, suddenly remember that he had not yet bought a gift for his wife's birthday, which he thinks (mistakenly) is two days hence. This also evokes a concern about not having paid his state taxes on time.

Remedies: full entries in a frequently consulted pocket notebook (names, addresses, phone numbers, projected events) and other mnemonic necessities, including preparation of manuscripts in large print to be read during forthcoming speeches formerly presented spontaneously.

Metapsychology

In my clinical (and personal) experience another phenomenon of aging is a tendency toward arcane thought and conduct. For instance, Wednesday may be considered a "fortunate" day for various enterprises, whereas on Friday (the day God created Adam and destined him for trouble?) one must be wary. Certainly, Friday is not a time when Schubert's "Death and the Maiden" is to be played if one's wife or daughter is ill. On reflection, such thoughts are dismissed as rank superstitions—yet Schubert's song is not hummed nor is the quartette played. Other examples of the mystically wishful or wry: At age fifty-five Auguste Comte, founder of sociology, began to believe that his deceased wife Clothilde had become Queen of Heaven, from where she directed his writings; Werner Heisenberg, genius of cosmic quantum mathematics, tacked a silvered horseshoe upright above his door as a uterine symbol of Venus—the goddess, not the planet.

Music

A personal account may be of interest to others devoted to this ethereal esthetic. From adolescence on, I studied, played and tried to compose music; now, as other pursuits falter, music partially takes their place. However, aging also takes its toll in some essentials:

Hearing. As noted above, neural receptors (cochleae) in each inner ear no longer effectively transmit high-frequency (treble) sounds to the brain, thereby depriving the listener of the enchanting harmonics above the basic tones of many musical instruments. This has had two personal effects: a compulsive retuning of my violins and viola to precise pitch, and a delight in the purity of chamber music as contrasted with the often clashing complexity of orchestral concerts —a preference also characteristic of aging composers.

Vision. Vagueness to the point of uneasy distinctions among notes marked flat, sharp or natural makes it difficult to read concentrated scores rapidly enough to maintain the required tempo; ergo, scrutinize and try to memorize polychromatic composers.

Mnemonics. Frequently throughout the day a musical theme invades consciousness, sometimes with odd variations. The sprightly opening bars of Mozart's "Hunt Quartette" may fade into the trivial "I've Got Spurs That Jingle, Jangle, Jingle" which, for no perceptible reason other than relief, is succeeded by some deeply reflective Beethoven adagio. Or I might hasten to jot down a supposedly original melody, later to remember it as part of a medieval motet. Conversely, musical memory can become pixyish; once, when I was asked at a party in my home to play some songs I had written, I could not recall their keys or development until I consulted their published versions.

Technique. Finger placements become less firm and accurate, trills are slowed and double harmonics are missed; worse, bowing loses flow, grace and expressiveness. The Mendelsohn Concerto may still be played with marginal satisfaction, but not the Brahms and certainly not the Tchaikovsky.

Solution. Enough daily practice to retard ossification; memorize compositions compatible with remaining skills; join a chamber group, preferably as an ever needed violist; and avoid solo performances other than before tolerant friends.

Physical Geriatrics

Strength. Each year books and chairs seem heavier, stairsteps higher and city blocks longer. Depending on heart-lung capacities, tennis may have to be confined to single-set doubles, and long jogging replaced by ruminative strolls. Substitutes: moderate, but regular, exercises at home.

Recreations. Golf can be retained, but as scores mount and partners desert, foursomes become onesomes, and no one is left to witness a miraculous hole in one. Sailing can often be continued, but since sails and anchors become unaccountably difficult to raise, Sea Scouts and other young deckhands can be invited on cruises "to learn how to sail." And, if a boat is chartered for a winter week or two on some southern sea, the arrangements should include provisions for an able-bodied bosun to act as cook and crew.

Travel. Extended and arduous foreign excursions should also be reined in. Invitations to faraway places may be respectfully declined primarily because the renewal of friendships in distant lands no longer compensates for long hours of discomfort in planes, trains and buses headed toward now familiar places—where, parenthetically, unfamiliar viruses lurk and where hovering renal or cardiac failures could not receive the care available at home. Instead, overseas friends are reciprocally offered hospitable receptions at homes here.

True, aging variably impairs nearly everyone's capacity to cope with traumatic disappointments and disillusionments, but excessively adverse reactions may be averted or alleviated by resorting to the comforts and reassurances also directly or tangentially described in this book. Among them: retrospective satisfactions derived from past tasks well accomplished, duties fulfilled and rewards received; retained talents, skills and creative activities; marital/familial securities and preserved friendships; confidence in some form of eternal existence either biologically through successive offspring, more subtly in generations of youth taught and inspired, and/or, theistically and transcendentally, faith in the possession of a deathless soul to be reincarnated on earth or to dwell forever in some rewarding heaven.

One of the most compelling reasons for believing in the existence of benign deities is that they have provided such sources of surcease to elderly readers of this book—and to its author.

Bibliography

Books by Dr. Masserman. Titles marked by an asterisk are written for general, as well as professional, readership.

1993   Writing and Editing the Humanities* (Amereon/Gardner)

1990   Psychiatric Consultations for Public Agencies
        (Charles C. Thomas)

1986   Psychiatry and Health* (Human Sciences Press)

1986   Technica Terapeuticas (Editorial Paidos)

1980   Principles and Practice of Biodynamic Psychotherapy
        (Thieme-Stratton)

1974   Psychiatric Syndromes and Modes of Therapy
        (Stratton Intercontinental)

1974   Terapia Dos Disturbios de Personalidade (José Olympio)

1973   Theory and Therapy in Dynamic Psychiatry
        (Jason Aronson)

1971   A Psychiatric Odyssey* (Science House)

1968   Biodynamic Roots of Human Behavior *with Victor Uribe, M.D.*
        (Charles C. Thomas)

1966   Modern Therapy of Personality Disorders (Wm. C. Brown)

1964   Behavior and Neurosis. Revised and expanded. (Hafner)

1955   Practice of Dynamic Psychiatry (W. B. Saunders)

1946   Principles of Dynamic Psychiatry (W.B. Saunders)

1943   Behavior and Neurosis (University of Chicago Press)

Dr. Masserman has also authored over three hundred articles on neurology, history, music, philosophy, esthetics and religion, produced more than thirty teaching films on neurotic behavior (including alcoholism) and published various musical compositions.

Co-Authored/Edited By Dr. Masserman

(Unless otherwise indicated, Dr. Masserman is senior author/editor.)

1993   Social Psychiatry and World Accords* *with Christine McGuire Masserman* (Amereon/Gardner)

1989   Adolescent Sexuality* with Victor Uribe, M.D. (Charles C. Thomas)

1986   Principios y Practica de la Psicoterpia Biodinamica with Victor Uribe, M.D. (Tercer Mundo)

1974   The Psychiatric Examination *with John Schwab, M.D.* (Stratton Intercontinental)

1972   Man for Humanity* *with John Schwab, M.D.* (Charles C. Thomas)

1962   Modern Concepts of Psychoanalysis* *with Leon Salzman, M.D., senior editor* (Philosophical Library)

1957-60 Progress in Psychotherapy. *Annual volumes, with J. L. Moreno* (Grune & Stratton)

Edited by Dr. Masserman

1961-83 Current Psychiatric Therapies. *Annual volumes.*
(Grune & Stratton)

1976 Social Psychiatry: The Range of Normal Behavior
(Grune & Stratton)

1956-72 Science and Psychoanalysis. *Annual volumes.*
(Grune & Stratton)

1969 Youth: A Transcultural Approach (Grune & Stratton)

1968 Psychiatry East and West (Grune & Stratton)

1966 Handbook of Psychiatric Therapies (Science House)

1959 Biological Psychiatry (Grune & Stratton)

1949 The Neuroses (Grune & Stratton)

Books co-authored/edited by Christine McGuire Masserman

In Press International Handbook of Medical Education *with*
A. Sajid, R. Veach, and Laura Aziz (Greenwood Press)

1983 Handbook of Health Professions Education *with R.P. Foley,*
A. Gorr and R. W. Richards (Jossey-Bass)

1976 Roles and Functions of Child Psychiatrists *with J.F.*
McDermott, Jr., M.D., senior editor, and E.S. Berner
(American Board of Psychiatry and Neurology)

1976 Clinical Simulations: Selected Problems in Patient
Management *with L.M. Solomon, M.D. and P. M. Forman,*
M.D. (Appleton-Century)

1968 A Review of the Nature and Use of Examinations in Medical
Education, available in French, Spanish, English & Russian
with J. Charvat and V. Parsons (World Health Organization)

Supplementary Readings

Berendzen, Richard and Laura A. Palmer. *A Man Overcomes the Tragic Aftermath of Childhood Sexual Abuse.* New York: Village Books, 1993. Mr. Berendzen, dismissed as president of American University for making obscene calls to child care workers, glibly attributes this compulsion to early sexual abuse by a psychotic mother.

Bernal, J. D. *Origin of Life.* London: Weidenfeld, 1967. Physiochemical theories imbued with vitality.

Billingham, John, ed. *Life in the Universe.* Cambridge, MA : MIT Press, 1981. A cosmic projection of mankind's yearnings for universality.

Bjerklie, David, Barry Hillenbrand and James O. Gottingen. "How Did Life Begin?" *Time,* October 11, 1993, pp. 68-74. Speculations extensively popularized.

Boas, Franz. *The Mind of Primitive Man.* NY: Macmillan, 1938. The intuitive insights of a pioneer anthropologist.

Burch, Claire. *Stranger In The Family: A Guide to Living with the Emotionally Disturbed.* Bobbs Merrill, 1972. Updated and Reissued Oakland, CA: Regent Press, 1994. This manual is the most objective, clear, concise and well informed compendium of advice and explanation to families on how to best understand behaviorally disturbed relatives and friends that I have ever read.

Dobzhansky, Theodosius, et al. *Evolution.* San Francisco: Freeman, 1977. Modified versions of Darwinism.

Dyson, F. *In Praise of Diversity.* New York: Science Press, 1988. Nuclear physics: philosophic, social and theologic implications.

Ehrenwald, J. *Psychotherapy, Myth and Method.* New York: Grune & Stratton, 1954. Applicable to current myths.

Fairstein, Linda A. *Sexual Violence: Twenty Years in New York's Sex Crimes Prosecuting Unit.* New York: William Morrow & Co., 1993. No sweeping generalizations.

Flowers, B.S. *The Power of Myth.* New York: Doubleday, 1987. What we live by.

Folsome, Clair Edwin. *The Origin of Life.* San Francisco: Freeman, 1979. A varied elaboration of the brief overview in the text.

Franz, Marie-Louise von. *Creation Myths.* Dallas: Spring, 1972. Intriguing approaches to mankind's seekings for identity.

Freund, Philip. *Myths of Creation.* London: Allen and Unwin, 1964. A comparative anthology.

Friedan, B. *The Fountain of Age.* New York: Simon and Schuster, 1993. A predictable apology for, and defense of, aging, with commentary on sexuality.

Friedman, L.M. *The Legal System: A Social Science Perspective.* New York: Russel Sage Foundation, 1992. Its virtues, vicissitudes and vices.

Gardner, H. *The Mind's New Science.* New York: Basic Books, 1975. Computer cognition.

Gulf News, United Arab Emirates. November 30, 1993. A married woman, mother of three and seven months pregnant, was arrested for adultery and sentenced by a traditional Muslim religious court to three hundred lashes and two years in prison; her lover was sentenced to ninety lashes, seven months in prison and deportation. On appeal, their sentences were reduced to ninety lashes and exile.

Jaroff, L. "Lies of the Mind." *Time,* November 20, 1993.
   A documented and predominantly unfavorable review of the
   trend among inept lay and professional mental health
   counselors to attribute "multiple personalities" and other
   behavioral aberrations to "repressed" experiences of childhood
   sexual abuse, thereby further confusing the patient's or
   "client's" conduct.

Jastrow, R. *God and the Astronomers.* New York: W.W. Norton,
   1978. A cosmologist's uncertainties.

Kaufman, W. *A Critique of Religion and Philosophy.* New York:
   Harper, 1958. A theologian's uncertainties.

Leakey, R.E. *Origins.* New York: Dutton, 1977. Genesis according to
   Dr. Leakey.

Morris, G.W. and Waters, T.J. *The Ordeal of Thomas Waters-
   Rimmer.* New York: William Morrow and Co., 1993.
   Mr. Waters recounts his sexual abuse by a pedophilic foster
   father and his suit against a child care agency that had subjected
   him to this ordeal.

Newsweek. "Sexual Correctness." October 5, 1993.
   Multi-authored, multifaceted, multi-contradictory critiques.
   Page 6 of this issue reports that a Stanford cheerleader dressed
   as a tree to minimize sex appeal.

Parinder, G. *World Religions.* New York: Facts Filled Publications,
   1971. Non-analytic, but inclusive, richly illustrated.

Pincherle, M. *An Illustrated History of Music.* New York: Reynal and
   Co., 1959. Interestingly scored.

Roehgeb, C.L. *Abstracts of the Standard Edition of Freud.*
   Washington, D.C.: National Institute of Mental Health, 1986.
   For Freudian scholars and critics.

Roiphe, Katie. *The Morning After: Sex, Fear and Feminism on
   Campus.* Boston: Little, Brown & Co., 1993. Poorly written, but
   frank and explanatory.

Schwab, J. and Schwab, M. *Sociocultural Roots of Mental Illness.* New York: Plenum, 1978. Ethnic, economic and cultural determinants.

Schmidt, W. *The Origin and Growth of Religion.* New York: Humanities Press, 1933. A classical treatise.

Sadock, M., Kaplan, H. and Freedman, A. *The Sexual Experience.* New York: Williams & Wilkins, 1976. Personally individualized, socioculturally variable.

About the Contributors

Christine McGuire Masserman, Professor Emerita, University of Illinois College of Medicine, has served as consultant to the World Health Organization, numerous medical schools and specialty societies, including the American Psychiatric Association, and is a trustee of the Foundation for International Accords.

Claire Burch has written widely recommended books on social issues including *Stranger in the Family,* described by reviewers as "a classic on caring for emotional disturbance." She is an independent filmmaker and is currently executive director of Art and Education Media. Her most recent book is *Homeless in the Nineties.*

Barbara Stackler is a highly trained and nationally known legal counselor, especially dedicated to the defense of the unjustly accused.